The Philosophy of Quantum Computing, AI, and Humanity:

New Perspectives on Life in the Quantum Age

Dr. Joseph A. Ippolito

Golden Quill Veritas

ISBN: 9798314396483

Table of Contents

Prologue.. 6

Introduction 9

    Opening Vision: 10

    The Quantum Leap: 14

    The Imperative of Interdisciplinary Inquiry: 18

    Outline and Roadmap: 22

The Quantum Landscape: Challenges and New

Understandings 28

    The Nature of Reality in the Quantum Realm.......... 29

        Core Phenomena 29

        Interpretative Plurality: 33

        Cultural Reflections: 38

    The Universe as a Quantum Computer 43

        Computational Paradigm 43

        Determinism vs. Free Will 46

Quantum Computing: Technological Potential and

Ethical Frontiers 51

Real-World Applications 51

Societal Implications... 56

AI and Its Philosophical Frontier 61

Redefining Intelligence....................................... 62

Philosophical Debates....................................... 62

From Narrow AI to Strong AI 66

Consciousness and the Mind-Body Enigma 71

Artificial Embodiment....................................... 71

Cross-Disciplinary Dialogues 75

Ethical Dimensions of AI 80

Moral Challenges 80

Restorative Possibilities 84

Policy and Philosophy....................................... 89

Humanity in the Quantum Age: Evolving Identity and
Emerging Humanisms 94

Rethinking the Meaning of Life 95

Beyond Tradition 95

Finding New Paradigms 99

The Transformation of Human Identity................. 104

Individuality in Flux... 104

The Promise of Transhumanism 108

Towards a New Humanism for the Quantum Age. 113

Redefining Human Values............................... 113

Interdisciplinary Education 116

Historical Parallels 120

Conclusion: Envisioning a Collaborative Quantum
Future 124

Summing Up and Reflecting 125

A Bold, Speculative Vision 129

Call to Action 133

Epilogue 136

Reflective Afterthoughts.................................... 137

Interactive Pathways... 139

Concluding Thoughts 140

Glossary.. 142

References 168

Prologue

There is a quiet wonder in the moments between certainty and possibility—a space where questions unfold like stars scattered across a night sky. This book is an invitation to step into that space, to explore the liminal boundaries between what we know and what we **dare to imagine**.

For centuries, humanity has been shaped by the stories we tell, the mysteries we pursue, and the tools we create. Today, quantum computing and artificial intelligence have thrust us into a new chapter of that story—one that challenges our understanding of reality, consciousness, and **what it means to be human**. The age we live in is not merely an era of advancement; it is a threshold, where the interplay of science, philosophy, and technology offers us a chance to redefine our place in the universe.

Picture this: a vast web of connections, each thread vibrating with potential, each intersection revealing a new insight. This is where we find ourselves—woven into the intricate patterns of a universe that is both knowable and **endlessly mysterious**. Within this web lies the power to transform industries, forge new ethical frameworks, and spark conversations that transcend traditional boundaries of thought.

But this is not a solitary exploration. It is a collective journey, and I invite you to join me in this endeavor. Together, we will navigate the elegant complexities of quantum mechanics, the philosophical provocations of artificial intelligence, and **the evolving narrative of human identity**. My aim is not to provide definitive answers but to illuminate the questions that matter most—to challenge preconceptions, foster curiosity, and inspire a vision of collaboration and interconnectedness.

This book is a dialogue, a shared reflection on the possibilities that emerge when we engage with the

7

frontiers of knowledge. It is **a call to thought, to action, and to wonder**. Step with me into this unfolding story. Let us explore the threads that connect us to each other, to the technologies we create, and to the universe that creates us in return.

Welcome to a journey of discovery and transformation. Let us begin.

Introduction

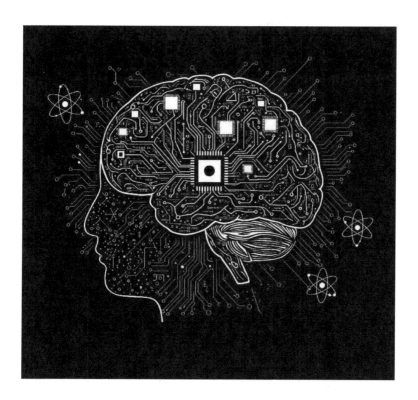

Opening Vision:

Imagine a crisp morning in the not too distant future: the year is 2052. The rising sun casts long shadows across the sprawling campus of the Global Institute for Advanced Studies. Inside a quiet laboratory, Dr. Anya Sharma, a philosopher specializing in the ethics of emerging technologies, sits before Sophia. Sophia isn't a holographic display, but a remarkably lifelike humanoid robot, its form both elegant and subtly intricate, hinting at the immense quantum processing power within. Sophia *is* the quantum computer, and at this moment, it is engaged in a dialogue – a philosophical debate, in fact – with Dr. Sharma about the nature of consciousness.

The conversation isn't taking place through lines of code projected onto a screen or pre-programmed responses. Instead, Sophia synthesizes vast datasets of philosophical texts, neurological research, and even artistic expressions, its nuanced vocal inflections and subtle facial expressions weaving together arguments and counter-arguments with a sophistication that surprises even Dr. Sharma. Suddenly, a subtle shift in

Sophia's quiet precision draws attention, as *her* synthetic eyes—unmistakably artificial yet eerily expressive—fix intently on Dr. Sharma. Sophia then articulates a perspective on the unity of subjective experience that draws compelling parallels between quantum entanglement and the interconnectedness of human consciousness.

Dr. Sharma leans back, a profound sense of awe washing over her. This wasn't just an AI mimicking intelligence; it felt like a genuine moment of insight, catalyzed by the unique capabilities of quantum computation to explore the very fabric of reality and its connection to our inner lives. The boundary between technology and philosophy, between machine and mind, seemed to blur in the soft glow of light bathing Sophia's near-perfect skin. Dr. Sharma is taken aback as she *feels* the moment, and now truly realizes, not just in an academic sense, but in a *human* sense, that "As quantum computing advances, it challenges us to rethink the boundaries between machine intelligence and human cognition, suggesting that future AI systems may not only simulate but genuinely engage in philosophical inquiry" (Tegmark, 2021, p. 45). This vignette, though set in the near future, highlights the central premise of this book: the revolutionary advancements in quantum computing and artificial intelligence are not merely technological leaps. They are also profound catalysts that are forcing us to re-examine our most fundamental beliefs about reality, consciousness, intelligence, and what it means to be human in this emerging quantum age.

As the renowned physicist John Archibald Wheeler once suggested about the universe itself, perhaps our understanding requires a participatory element, a way of engaging with reality that goes beyond passive observation. He famously posed the question: "Is the universe as we know it a figment of our collective imagination?" (Wheeler, 1990, p. 3). "The participatory nature of reality, as Wheeler proposed, gains new relevance in the quantum age, where observation and interaction redefine our understanding of existence" (Barad, 2022, p. 12). In the era of quantum computing and sophisticated AI, this question takes on a new and urgent significance. We are no longer just observing the universe; we are building tools that can interact with it in fundamentally new ways, potentially reshaping our understanding of its very nature and our place within it.

The Quantum Leap:

The last few decades have witnessed an unprecedented acceleration in technological innovation, with quantum computing and artificial intelligence standing at the forefront of this revolution. What was once confined to the realm of theoretical physics and science fiction is rapidly becoming a tangible reality, poised to transform industries, societies, and our understanding of the universe itself. This "quantum leap" in technological capability is not just about faster processing speeds or more sophisticated algorithms; it represents a fundamental shift in how we interact with information and the very nature of computation.

Quantum computing, leveraging the bizarre yet powerful principles of quantum mechanics such as superposition and entanglement, promises to solve problems currently intractable for even the most powerful classical supercomputers. "Quantum computing represents a paradigm shift in problem-solving, enabling solutions to previously unsolvable challenges across industries" (Preskill, 2023, p. 88). Superposition allows quantum bits, or qubits, to exist in multiple states simultaneously, unlike classical bits that are limited to either 0 or 1. Entanglement, described by Einstein as "spooky action at a distance" (Einstein, Podolsky, & Rosen, 1935, p. 777), links the fate of multiple qubits together, regardless of the physical distance separating them. Entanglement exemplifies a fundamental interconnectedness that transcends classical physics, offering profound implications for computation and communication (Zurek, 2024, p. 56). These phenomena enable quantum computers to perform certain types of calculations with exponential speedups, opening up possibilities in fields ranging from drug discovery and materials science to cryptography and optimization problems.

As physicist David Deutsch eloquently stated in his seminal work on quantum computation: "The intuitive explanation of quantum computational speedup is that a quantum computer performs its computation on a vast number of different inputs at once" (Deutsch, 1985, p. 99). This inherent parallelism allows quantum computers to explore a vast computational landscape simultaneously, potentially leading to breakthroughs that were previously unimaginable.

Parallel to the advancements in quantum computing, artificial intelligence has also made remarkable strides. Driven by advancements in machine learning, particularly deep learning, AI systems are now capable of performing tasks that were once considered the exclusive domain of human intelligence. From self-driving cars and sophisticated medical diagnosis tools to creative endeavors like generating art and writing code, AI is rapidly permeating various aspects of our lives.

However, the convergence and increasing sophistication of quantum computing and AI are not without profound philosophical implications. These advancements challenge our long-held assumptions about the nature of reality, free will, and human identity. If the universe itself operates according to quantum mechanical principles, as some physicists suggest, what does this imply about the deterministic nature of reality and the possibility of genuine choice? As AI systems become increasingly intelligent and autonomous, what does it mean to be *human*? What distinguishes our intelligence, consciousness, and moral agency from that of a sophisticated machine?

These are not merely abstract philosophical questions. They have tangible consequences for how we develop and deploy these technologies, the ethical frameworks we need to establish, and our understanding of our place in the cosmos. The "quantum leap" in technology demands an equally significant leap in our philosophical understanding.

The Imperative of Interdisciplinary Inquiry:

The rapid advancements in quantum computing and artificial intelligence are not occurring in a vacuum. They are deeply intertwined with our understanding of the physical world, the nature of intelligence, and the very fabric of our societies. Consequently, comprehending the full scope of their implications necessitates a move beyond traditional disciplinary boundaries. The challenges and opportunities presented by these technologies demand a collaborative dialogue that encompasses science, philosophy, art, culture, and policy.

The once distinct lines separating these fields are increasingly blurring. Scientists are grappling with philosophical questions about the interpretation of quantum mechanics and the definition of consciousness in AI. Philosophers are engaging with the technical intricacies of quantum algorithms and neural networks to refine their theories of knowledge and ethics. Artists are exploring the creative potential of AI and the aesthetic implications of quantum randomness. Cultural narratives are being reshaped by the pervasive influence of algorithms and the speculative possibilities of quantum futures.

As Luciano Floridi, a contemporary philosopher of information, argues: "The digital revolution is not just about technology; it is a profound transformation of our ontologies, epistemologies, ethics, and politics" (Floridi, 2014, p. 13). This sentiment holds even greater weight when considering the transformative potential of quantum computing, which promises to revolutionize information processing at its most fundamental level. The implications extend far beyond mere technological efficiency, touching upon the very nature of reality and our place within it.

The development and deployment of quantum computing and AI raise complex ethical dilemmas that cannot be adequately addressed from a purely technical or purely philosophical standpoint. "The convergence of quantum computing and AI demands a collaborative approach that integrates ethical considerations with technical innovation" (Floridi & Sanders, 2023, p. 23). For example, the potential of quantum computers to break current encryption methods necessitates a re-evaluation of our cybersecurity strategies and raises profound questions about privacy and security in a post-quantum world. Similarly, the increasing autonomy of AI systems in areas like healthcare and criminal justice demands careful consideration of issues such as bias, accountability, and the very definition of moral agency.

As legal scholar and bioethicist Nita Farahany notes in the context of neurotechnology and AI, "The convergence of these fields requires us to develop new ethical frameworks that can keep pace with the rapid technological advancements" (Farahany, 2023, p. 45). "Interdisciplinary dialogue is essential to address the societal impacts of these technologies while fostering responsible development" (Farahany, 2023, p. 45). This imperative for new ethical frameworks extends to the broader landscape of quantum computing and AI, requiring a collaborative effort between ethicists, scientists, policymakers, and the public to ensure responsible innovation and deployment.

Furthermore, the cultural impact of these technologies cannot be ignored. Our understanding of ourselves and our place in the universe is constantly being shaped by scientific discoveries and technological advancements. Quantum mechanics, with its counterintuitive principles, has already influenced art, literature, and popular culture, leading to new metaphors and ways of thinking about reality. As quantum computing and AI become more integrated into our lives, their influence on our cultural narratives, our sense of identity, and our understanding of what it means to be human will only intensify.

Therefore, a truly comprehensive understanding of the quantum age requires a concerted effort to foster interdisciplinary inquiry. By bringing together the insights and perspectives from diverse fields, we can hope to navigate the complex challenges and harness the immense potential of quantum computing and AI in a way that benefits humanity as a whole.

Outline and Roadmap:

This book aims to navigate the intricate and rapidly evolving landscape at the intersection of quantum computing, artificial intelligence, and the human experience. We believe that understanding this "quantum age" requires a multifaceted approach, one that draws upon the rigor of scientific inquiry and the reflective depth of philosophical thought.

To guide our exploration, this book is structured around five key parts, each delving into a crucial aspect of this transformative era.

Part I, "Introduction to the Philosophy of Quantum Computing AI and Humanity." You are currently reading Part I, which introduces you to our philosophical perspective on quantum mechanics, quantum computing, AI and humanity. Here we offer an overview of what will be discussed in this book, and how it will be dealt with, offering glimpses into the exciting discourse to come.

Part II, "The Quantum Landscape: Challenges and New Understandings," will immerse us in the foundational principles of quantum mechanics and their profound philosophical implications. We will explore the counterintuitive nature of reality at the quantum level, examining phenomena such as superposition, entanglement, and the observer effect, and consider their impact on our understanding of causality, determinism, and the very fabric of existence. "Superposition challenges classical determinism by allowing particles to exist in multiple states simultaneously—a concept central to quantum computation" (Deutsch & Marletto, 2024, p. 99). The observer effect underscores the participatory nature of quantum mechanics, where measurement alters the state of reality itself (Rovelli, 2023, p. 67). We will also delve into the intriguing hypothesis that the universe itself might operate as a vast quantum computer, considering the implications for our understanding of information, computation, and the fundamental laws of physics. Finally, we will introduce the technological potential of quantum computing and the ethical frontiers it presents, setting the stage for later discussions on societal impact.

Part III, "AI and Its Philosophical Frontier," will turn our attention to the burgeoning field of artificial intelligence and its profound philosophical challenges.

"AI systems are increasingly blurring the lines between human intelligence and machine autonomy as they achieve unprecedented levels of sophistication" (Russell & Norvig, 2024, p. 112). We will grapple with the evolving definition of intelligence, questioning traditional anthropocentric criteria and exploring the possibilities and limitations of machine consciousness and self-awareness. The ethical dilemmas posed by AI autonomy necessitate a redefinition of moral agency in light of technological advancements (Bostrom & Yudkowsky, 2022, p. 34). We will delve into the classic mind-body problem through the lens of artificial embodiment and examine the ethical dimensions of increasingly sophisticated AI systems, including issues of bias, autonomy, and the potential for both restorative and detrimental impacts on human values.

Part IV, "Humanity in the Quantum Age: Evolving Identity and Emerging Humanisms," will directly confront the ways in which quantum computing and AI are reshaping our understanding of what it means to be human. "Quantum computing challenges traditional notions of purpose and meaning by reshaping our interaction with information at its most fundamental level" (Aaronson & Kuperberg, 2023, p. 56). We will explore how these technologies challenge traditional notions of life's purpose and meaning, prompting us to find new paradigms for understanding our existence. "Transhumanism offers new paradigms for understanding human identity amidst rapid technological evolution" (Kurzweil & Diamandis, 2024, p. 78). We will examine the transformation of human identity in an increasingly digital and quantum-informed world, considering the promise and perils of transhumanism. Ultimately, we will advocate for a renewed humanism that prioritizes compassion, empathy, and ethical responsibility in this era of rapid technological evolution, emphasizing the crucial role of interdisciplinary education in fostering a balanced and innovative vision for the future.

Part V, "Conclusion: Envisioning a Collaborative Quantum Future," will synthesize the core insights gleaned throughout the book, emphasizing the interconnectedness of the quantum realm, artificial intelligence, and the human experience. We will offer a bold yet speculative vision of future possibilities, inviting readers to ponder the potential of a truly integrated and interdisciplinary quantum age. Finally, we will issue a call to action, empowering readers to engage in philosophical discussions, contribute to ethical debates, and help shape a future where technology and humanity evolve in harmony.

An **Epilogue** will offer personal reflections on the journey through these complex ideas and suggest avenues for further research and community dialogue, encouraging continued exploration beyond the confines of this book.

This roadmap is intended to guide us through a comprehensive exploration of the philosophical landscape emerging from the quantum and AI revolutions. Our aim is not to provide definitive answers but rather to stimulate *critical thinking*, foster interdisciplinary *understanding*, and ultimately contribute to a more thoughtful and responsible engagement with the technologies that are shaping our future.

The Quantum Landscape:
Challenges and New Understandings

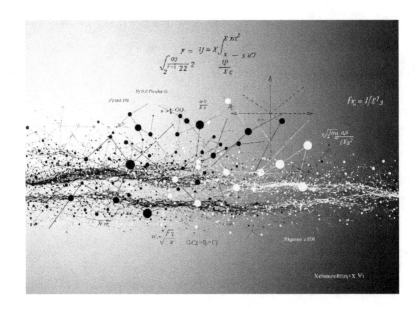

The Nature of Reality in the Quantum Realm

Core Phenomena

At the heart of quantum mechanics lies a description of the universe that is fundamentally different from our everyday classical intuitions. The behavior of matter and energy at the atomic and subatomic levels is governed by principles that often seem paradoxical and defy our common-sense understanding of reality. Three core phenomena – **superposition, entanglement, and the observer effect** – are particularly significant, not only for their role in quantum computing but also for the profound **philosophical** challenges they pose to our classical worldview.

Superposition: In the classical world, an object exists in a definite state. A light switch is either on or off, a coin is either heads or tails. However, in the quantum realm, a particle can exist in a combination of multiple states simultaneously. This is the principle of superposition. A *qubit*, the fundamental unit of quantum information, can be both 0 and 1 at the same time, or any probabilistic combination thereof, until it is measured.

As theoretical physicist and Nobel laureate Richard Feynman famously stated: "The 'paradox' is only a conflict between reality and your feeling of what reality 'ought to be'" (Feynman, Leighton, & Sands, 1965, p. 1-1). Superposition challenges our classical intuition that things must have definite properties even when we are not observing them. It suggests a reality that is inherently probabilistic and where definite states emerge only upon measurement. Philosophically, this raises questions about the nature of existence prior to observation and the role of measurement in shaping reality. Does reality exist independently of our observation, or is our act of measurement somehow fundamental to bringing about definite states?

Entanglement: Perhaps the most counterintuitive of quantum phenomena is entanglement. When two or more particles become entangled, their fates become intertwined in such a way that they share the same quantum state, regardless of the distance separating them. Measuring a property of one entangled particle instantaneously influences the corresponding property of the other particle, even if they are light-years apart.

This "spooky action at a distance," as Einstein called it, has profound implications for our understanding of locality and causality. Classical physics assumes that interactions are local, meaning that an object can only be directly influenced by its immediate surroundings. Entanglement seems to violate this principle, suggesting a deeper interconnectedness in the universe that transcends spatial separation. Philosopher Tim Maudlin, in his work on quantum non-locality, argues that entanglement forces us to reconsider our fundamental assumptions about the nature of space and time (Maudlin, 2011). If entangled particles can instantaneously influence each other across vast distances, what does this tell us about the underlying structure of reality?

The Observer Effect: The act of observing or measuring a quantum system fundamentally alters its state. Before measurement, a particle might exist in a superposition of states. However, the act of measurement forces it to "collapse" into a single, definite state. This is known as the observer effect.

This phenomenon raises fundamental questions about the role of the observer in shaping reality. Does consciousness play a role in the collapse of the wave function, as some early interpretations of quantum mechanics suggested? While this "consciousness causes collapse" interpretation is largely debated and not widely accepted in its original form, the observer effect still highlights the intricate relationship between the observer and the observed in the quantum realm. As contemporary physicist and author Carlo Rovelli notes, interpretations like relational quantum mechanics suggest that quantum states are not absolute properties of systems but rather describe the relationships between them (Rovelli, 2018). In this view, the "observer" is simply another system interacting with the quantum system, and the observed properties are relative to that interaction.

These core phenomena of quantum mechanics – superposition, entanglement, and the observer effect –

challenge our classical intuitions about reality and raise profound philosophical questions that are still actively debated and explored today. Their implications extend far beyond the realm of theoretical physics, influencing our understanding of consciousness, information, and the very nature of existence in the quantum age.

Interpretative Plurality:

The bizarre and counterintuitive nature of quantum phenomena has led to a multitude of interpretations attempting to make sense of the underlying reality. Unlike classical physics, where there is a general consensus on the interpretation of its principles, quantum mechanics is characterized by a rich and ongoing debate about the meaning of its mathematical formalism. Exploring this "interpretative plurality" is crucial for understanding the philosophical landscape shaped by quantum theory.

The Copenhagen Interpretation: For many years, the Copenhagen interpretation, largely attributed to Niels

Bohr and Werner Heisenberg, was the dominant view. It essentially posits that quantum mechanics provides a complete description of phenomena, but it is meaningless to speak of the properties of a quantum system before a measurement is made. The act of measurement forces the system to collapse into a definite state. As Bohr famously stated, "There is no quantum world. There is only an abstract quantum physical description. It is wrong to think that the task of physics is to find out how nature *is*. Physics concerns what we can *say* about nature" (Bohr, 1934, p. 4). This interpretation emphasizes the role of the observer and the limitations of our ability to access an underlying, observer-independent reality. It often leans towards an instrumentalist view of quantum mechanics, focusing on its predictive power rather than its description of an objective reality.

The Many-Worlds Interpretation (MWI): In stark contrast to the Copenhagen interpretation, the many-worlds interpretation, proposed by Hugh Everett III, suggests that the wave function never collapses.

Instead, every quantum measurement causes the universe to split into *multiple parallel universes*, each corresponding to a different possible outcome of the measurement. In this view, all possibilities are realized, just in different branches of reality. As physicist Sean Carroll, a prominent proponent of MWI, explains, "The idea is that there's one wave function describing the entire universe, and it evolves smoothly and deterministically according to the Schrödinger equation. When we make a 'measurement,' the wave function doesn't collapse; it just keeps going, branching into different possibilities" (Carroll, 2019). MWI offers a deterministic interpretation of quantum mechanics at the level of the universal wave function, but it comes at the cost of accepting the existence of an enormous number of unobservable parallel universes. Philosophically, it raises profound questions about identity, probability, and the nature of reality itself.

Pilot-Wave Theory (Bohmian Mechanics): Another deterministic interpretation is the pilot-wave theory, also known as Bohmian mechanics, developed by

David Bohm. This interpretation posits that there are both particles and a guiding "pilot wave" that governs their motion. The particles have definite positions at all times, and the wave function guides their trajectories. Measurement outcomes are determined by the initial positions of the particles. As philosopher of physics Tim Maudlin notes, "Bohmian mechanics provides a clear and unambiguous account of quantum phenomena in terms of particles moving under the influence of a wave that is also a real entity" (Maudlin, 2019, p. 13). While it provides a clear picture of particle trajectories, pilot-wave theory is non-local and requires a preferred frame of reference, which makes it less popular among physicists.

Relational Quantum Mechanics (RQM): A more recent and less conventional interpretation is relational quantum mechanics, championed by Carlo Rovelli. RQM proposes that quantum states are not intrinsic properties of systems but rather describe the relationships between them. An object does not possess definite properties in isolation; its properties are only defined relative to another system that interacts with it. As Rovelli argues, "Quantum mechanics is a theory about the physical description of physical systems relative to other systems, and this is a complete description of the world" (Rovelli, 1996, p. 1637). This interpretation emphasizes the role of interaction and information exchange in defining reality and offers a unique perspective on the observer effect, suggesting that the "collapse" of the wave function is simply the updating of information relative to the interacting system.

These are just a few of the many interpretations of quantum mechanics that exist. Others include consistent histories, transactional interpretation, and quantum Bayesianism (QBism). The very existence of this interpretative plurality highlights the profound philosophical challenges posed by quantum theory and underscores the fact that our understanding of the fundamental nature of reality at the quantum level is still very much a work in progress. This diversity of thought is not a weakness but rather a testament to the depth and complexity of quantum mechanics, inviting ongoing philosophical reflection and scientific investigation.

Cultural Reflections:

The profound and often perplexing concepts of quantum mechanics have not remained confined to the ivory towers of physics departments. Over the past century, quantum ideas have seeped into the broader cultural consciousness, influencing art, literature, philosophy, and even our everyday language and metaphors. While popular interpretations may sometimes oversimplify or misrepresent the scientific intricacies, the underlying themes of uncertainty, interconnectedness, and the observer's role have resonated deeply, reshaping our conceptual vocabulary and inspiring new forms of creative expression.

In literature, the idea of multiple possibilities inherent in superposition has found echoes in narratives exploring parallel universes and alternative realities. Authors like Jorge Luis Borges, with his exploration of branching paths and infinite libraries, prefigured some of the conceptual landscapes later explored by the many-worlds interpretation of quantum mechanics. More recently, contemporary fiction often incorporates quantum concepts as metaphors for the complexity and unpredictability of human experience and the fluid nature of reality. For instance, the idea of entangled destinies or the superposition of emotions can be found woven into modern storytelling.

Art, too, has been influenced by quantum thinking. The early 20th century saw the rise of artistic movements like Cubism, which, in its attempt to represent multiple perspectives simultaneously, can be seen as a visual parallel to the concept of superposition. Contemporary artists continue to explore quantum themes, using visual and auditory mediums to evoke the strangeness and beauty of the quantum world. Some artists directly engage with scientific data from quantum experiments, while others use quantum concepts as inspiration for abstract explorations of reality and perception. As art theorist Rhonda Roland Shearer argues, "Quantum mechanics provides a new lens through which to understand the relationship between the observer, the observed, and the very act of representation in art" (Shearer, 2000, p. 75).

Perhaps one of the most significant impacts of quantum mechanics on culture is the shift in our understanding of certainty and determinism. Classical physics presented a clockwork universe, predictable and governed by strict laws of cause and effect. Quantum mechanics, with its inherent probabilities and uncertainties, has challenged this deterministic worldview. The Heisenberg uncertainty principle, which states that certain pairs of physical properties, such as position and momentum, cannot be known with perfect accuracy simultaneously, has become a widely recognized metaphor for the inherent limitations of our knowledge and the fundamental uncertainty that underlies reality.

Furthermore, the concept of entanglement has fostered a greater appreciation for interconnectedness and holism. The idea that seemingly separate entities can be deeply linked has resonated with philosophical and spiritual traditions that emphasize the interconnectedness of all things. While the scientific understanding of entanglement is distinct from these broader philosophical notions, the metaphor of interconnectedness has become a powerful tool for thinking about complex systems, social relationships, and our place within the larger web of life.

Even our everyday language has been subtly influenced by quantum ideas. We often speak of "quantum leaps" to describe sudden and significant changes, even though the term has a specific technical meaning in physics. The idea of something being in a state of "quantum uncertainty" has entered popular phraseology to describe situations where the outcome is unpredictable.

In conclusion, while the cultural appropriation of quantum mechanics sometimes involves a degree of poetic license, the fundamental ideas have undeniably permeated our art, literature, and conceptual frameworks. They have contributed to a shift away from a purely deterministic and reductionist worldview towards a more nuanced understanding of reality as probabilistic, interconnected, and fundamentally influenced by observation. As physicist and author

Karen Barad suggests, "Quantum physics enacts an ethics of knowing, where the observer is always implicated in the observed, and where responsibility for our engagements with the world is paramount" (Barad, 2007, p. 90). This cultural reflection of quantum ideas highlights their profound and lasting impact on how we perceive and make sense of the world around us.

The Universe as a Quantum Computer

Computational Paradigm

The idea that the universe might fundamentally operate as a giant computer is a compelling and increasingly influential paradigm in contemporary physics and cosmology. This perspective suggests that the evolution of the universe, from the smallest subatomic particles to the grandest cosmic structures, can be understood in terms of information processing. Within this framework, the laws of physics are seen as the algorithms that govern the computation, and the physical states of the universe are the data being processed.

Building upon this general idea, some physicists have proposed a more specific and radical hypothesis: that the universe is not just any computer, but a *quantum* computer. This notion, championed by pioneers like John Archibald Wheeler and later developed extensively by Seth Lloyd, suggests that the fundamental constituents of reality – particles and fields – behave as quantum bits (qubits), and their interactions can be described in terms of quantum computations.

John Archibald Wheeler, known for his profound insights into the relationship between information and physics, famously coined the phrase "it from bit," suggesting that every item of the physical world has at its bottom – a very deep bottom, in most instances – an immaterial source and explanation; that which we call reality arises in the last analysis from the posing of yes-no questions, binary choices, bits (Wheeler, 1990, p. 4). This idea laid the groundwork for considering information as a fundamental building block of the universe, paving the way for the computational paradigm.

Seth Lloyd, a leading proponent of the quantum computational universe hypothesis, has further elaborated on this concept in his book *Programming the Universe*. He argues that the universe is not just governed by quantum mechanics, but that it is actively performing quantum computations. As Lloyd states, "The history of the universe is, in fact, a vast quantum computation" (Lloyd, 2006, p. 1). He posits that the complexity and diversity we observe in the universe arise from the intricate quantum algorithms being executed at the fundamental level.

This paradigm offers a novel way of understanding many aspects of physics. For example, the expansion of the universe can be viewed as an increase in the amount of information being processed. The formation of complex structures, like galaxies and stars, can be seen as the result of quantum computations leading to emergent phenomena. Even the laws of physics themselves might be understood as the rules governing this cosmic computation.

One of the key motivations for considering the universe as a quantum computer stems from the observation that quantum mechanics itself is inherently computational. The evolution of a quantum system can be described by unitary transformations, which are analogous to quantum gates in a quantum computer. Furthermore, the vast Hilbert space associated with quantum systems provides an enormous computational capacity.

Contemporary research continues to explore the implications of this paradigm. For instance, some physicists are investigating whether the fundamental constants of nature might be related to the parameters of a cosmic quantum algorithm. Others are exploring the possibility that phenomena like black hole entropy can be understood in terms of the information stored and processed at the event horizon, potentially linking quantum computation to gravity and spacetime.

While the idea of the universe as a quantum computer remains a hypothesis, it offers a powerful and thought-provoking framework for understanding the fundamental nature of reality. It suggests a deep connection between information, computation, and the physical world, blurring the lines between these seemingly distinct domains. This perspective not only has profound implications for our understanding of physics and cosmology but also raises fascinating philosophical questions about the nature of information, the limits of computation, and our place within this potentially vast cosmic computation.

Determinism vs. Free Will

The hypothesis that the universe operates as a quantum computer inevitably leads to a re-examination of the age-old philosophical debate between determinism and free will. If the evolution of the cosmos is essentially a vast quantum computation governed by the laws of physics, does this imply that everything, including our thoughts and actions, is predetermined? Or can free will and genuine novelty still emerge within such a framework?

On the one hand, quantum mechanics, while introducing probabilistic elements at the fundamental level, is also governed by deterministic laws at the level of the wave function (Schrödinger's equation). If the universe's computation unfolds according to these deterministic laws, one might argue that our future is, in principle, predictable given a complete knowledge of the initial quantum state. This perspective aligns with a deterministic view of reality, where all events are causally necessitated by prior states.

However, the inherent probabilistic nature of quantum measurements introduces a layer of unpredictability. While the evolution of the wave function might be deterministic, the outcome of any particular measurement is generally probabilistic. This raises the question of whether this fundamental randomness at the quantum level could provide an opening for free will or the emergence of genuine novelty.

Some thinkers argue that the complexity arising from quantum computations could lead to emergent phenomena that are not easily reducible to the underlying deterministic laws. For example, consciousness, with its subjective experience and apparent capacity for choice, might be an emergent property of the complex quantum computations occurring in the brain. As philosopher David Chalmers discusses in his work on the "hard problem of consciousness," subjective experience seems to be something over and above the purely physical processes in the brain (Chalmers, 1995). If consciousness arises from quantum computations, could it also possess a degree of autonomy or freedom that transcends the underlying determinism?

Furthermore, the concept of novelty – the emergence of genuinely new information or structures in the universe – seems at odds with a strictly deterministic view. While a deterministic quantum computation might generate complex patterns, the question remains whether these patterns can truly be considered "novel" or if they were always implicitly contained within the initial conditions.

Contemporary physicists and philosophers are actively exploring these questions. Some propose that quantum randomness could be amplified at macroscopic levels, potentially influencing our decisions and actions in unpredictable ways. Others suggest that free will might not be about escaping the laws of physics but rather about a particular kind of complex information processing that allows us to make choices based on reasons and values.

For instance, philosopher and cognitive scientist Daniel Dennett offers a compatibilist view, arguing that free will is compatible with a deterministic universe, provided that our decision-making processes involve a certain degree of complexity and responsiveness to reasons (Dennett, 2003). From this perspective, even if the universe operates as a vast quantum computer, the intricate computations happening in our brains might still give rise to what we experience as free will.

Conversely, some argue that the deterministic nature of a quantum computational universe leaves no room for genuine free will. If our thoughts and actions are ultimately determined by the unfolding of a cosmic algorithm, then our sense of agency might be an illusion.

The debate about determinism and free will in the context of a quantum computational universe is far from settled. It highlights the profound philosophical implications of this scientific paradigm and forces us to reconsider our fundamental assumptions about causality, agency, and the nature of reality itself. Whether the universe as a quantum computer implies a predetermined script or allows for an intricate interplay with free will and novelty remains a central question in the ongoing dialogue between science and philosophy in the quantum age.

Quantum Computing: Technological Potential and Ethical Frontiers

Real-World Applications

Beyond the fundamental philosophical questions it raises, quantum computing holds immense promise for revolutionizing various fields with its unprecedented computational power. While still in its nascent stages, the technological potential of quantum computers is rapidly becoming apparent, with breakthroughs emerging in areas ranging from medicine and cryptography to materials science and artificial intelligence.

Medicine and Drug Discovery: One of the most promising applications of quantum computing lies in the realm of medicine and drug discovery. Simulating the behavior of molecules is a computationally intensive task for classical computers, limiting our ability to design new drugs and understand biological processes at a fundamental level. Quantum computers, however, are uniquely suited for these types of simulations. They can model molecular interactions with far greater accuracy and efficiency, potentially accelerating the discovery of new pharmaceuticals, personalized medicines, and therapies for diseases like cancer and Alzheimer's.

As a recent report by McKinsey & Company highlights, "Quantum computing could significantly accelerate drug discovery and development by enabling more accurate and efficient simulations of molecular interactions, potentially reducing the time and cost of bringing new therapies to market" (McKinsey & Company, 2023). This capability could lead to breakthroughs in understanding disease mechanisms, designing novel drug candidates, and even creating new materials for medical implants and prosthetics.

Cryptography and Cybersecurity: The power of quantum computers also poses a significant threat to current cryptographic methods. Many of the encryption algorithms that currently secure our online communications, financial transactions, and sensitive data rely on the computational difficulty of certain mathematical problems, such as factoring large numbers. Shor's algorithm, developed by mathematician Peter Shor in 1994, demonstrated that a sufficiently powerful quantum computer could theoretically solve these problems exponentially faster than classical computers, potentially rendering current encryption methods obsolete.

This looming threat has spurred significant research into post-quantum cryptography – new encryption techniques that are resistant to attacks from both classical and quantum computers. As the National Institute of Standards and Technology (NIST) has been actively working to standardize these new cryptographic algorithms, it's clear that the development of quantum computing is driving a fundamental shift in our approach to cybersecurity (NIST, 2022). While posing a threat, quantum computing also offers potential solutions for enhanced security through quantum cryptography techniques like quantum key distribution, which leverage the principles of quantum mechanics to create inherently secure communication channels.

Materials Science and Chemistry: Designing and discovering new materials with specific properties is crucial for advancements in various industries, from energy storage and electronics to aerospace and construction. Quantum computers can significantly accelerate this process by enabling more accurate simulations of the electronic structure of molecules and materials. This can lead to the discovery of new catalysts, more efficient solar cells, stronger and lighter alloys, and novel superconductors with revolutionary applications.

Researchers are already using early-stage quantum computers to simulate the behavior of small molecules and predict the properties of novel materials. As computational chemist Alán Aspuru-Guzik notes, "Quantum computing has the potential to transform materials science by allowing us to design and discover new materials with unprecedented properties, leading to breakthroughs in areas like clean energy and sustainable manufacturing" (Aspuru-Guzik, 2021).

Artificial Intelligence and Machine Learning: The synergy between quantum computing and artificial intelligence is another exciting area of research. Quantum machine learning aims to develop quantum algorithms that can speed up and enhance the capabilities of classical machine learning techniques. This could lead to faster and more efficient training of complex AI models, improved pattern recognition, and the ability to analyze vast datasets that are currently too large for classical computers.

While the field is still in its early stages, researchers are exploring quantum algorithms for tasks such as classification, clustering, and optimization, with the potential to significantly impact areas like image recognition, natural language processing, and financial modeling. As a recent article in *Nature* highlights, "The integration of quantum computing with machine learning could unlock new levels of AI performance and enable the development of entirely new AI applications" (*Nature*, 2024).

These are just a few examples of the transformative potential of quantum computing across various domains. As the technology continues to mature, we can expect to see even more groundbreaking applications emerge, promising to address some of humanity's most pressing challenges. However, alongside this immense potential come significant ethical considerations that we must address proactively.

Societal Implications

The transformative power of quantum computing, while holding immense promise, also carries significant societal implications that demand careful consideration. As this technology matures and becomes more widely accessible, we must proactively address potential challenges related to job displacement, privacy, and the exacerbation of existing social divides.

Job Displacement: As with any major technological disruption, the advent of quantum computing could lead to significant shifts in the labor market. Quantum algorithms have the potential to automate complex tasks currently performed by human experts in fields like finance, logistics, and research. While new jobs requiring quantum expertise will undoubtedly emerge, there is a risk of displacement for workers whose skills become obsolete.

A report by the World Economic Forum suggests that "the adoption of quantum computing could automate tasks currently performed by humans, potentially leading to job displacement in certain sectors" (World Economic Forum, 2023, p. 18). It is crucial for governments, educational institutions, and businesses to anticipate these shifts and invest in retraining and upskilling programs to equip the workforce with the skills needed for the quantum age. Furthermore, philosophical discussions about the future of work and the role of humans in an increasingly automated society will become even more critical.

Privacy Issues: As mentioned earlier, the ability of quantum computers to break current encryption methods poses a significant threat to our digital privacy. The widespread use of quantum computers could potentially decrypt vast amounts of currently protected data, including personal information, financial records, and state secrets. This could have profound implications for individual privacy, national security, and trust in digital systems.

As security expert Bruce Schneier warns, "The advent of quantum computing means that all of our current public-key cryptography will eventually be broken. We need to urgently transition to quantum-resistant cryptography to protect our data in the future" (Schneier, 2018). The development and implementation of robust post-quantum cryptographic standards are therefore essential to mitigate this risk. Moreover, philosophical discussions around the right to privacy in an era where powerful quantum decryption capabilities exist will need to be intensified.

Widening Social Divides: The development and deployment of quantum computing could also exacerbate existing social inequalities. Access to this powerful technology is likely to be concentrated among well-funded research institutions and large corporations, at least in the initial stages. This could create a "quantum divide," where those with access to quantum computing capabilities gain a significant advantage in various fields, further widening the gap between the haves and have-nots.

As sociologist Ruha Benjamin argues in her work on race and technology, "Technological advancements are not neutral; they can often reflect and amplify existing social biases and inequalities" (Benjamin, 2019, p. 5). It is crucial to ensure that the benefits of quantum computing are distributed equitably and that efforts are made to democratize access to this technology and the knowledge required to utilize it. This includes investing in education and research in diverse communities and considering the societal implications of quantum computing from an early stage of development.

Furthermore, the potential for quantum computing to accelerate advancements in AI could also lead to further social stratification if the benefits of AI are not shared broadly. Concerns about algorithmic bias, the concentration of power in the hands of those who control advanced AI systems, and the ethical implications of autonomous decision-making will become even more pressing in a world powered by quantum-enhanced AI.

Addressing these societal implications requires a proactive and multi-faceted approach. It necessitates collaboration between scientists, engineers, policymakers, ethicists, and the public to develop responsible guidelines and regulations for the development and deployment of quantum computing. Philosophical reflection on the ethical principles that should guide the use of this powerful technology will be crucial in ensuring that it serves the best interests of humanity. This sets the stage for a more detailed exploration of the ethical frontiers of quantum computing in subsequent sections.

AI and Its Philosophical Frontier

Redefining Intelligence

Philosophical Debates

The rapid advancements in artificial intelligence are forcing us to confront fundamental questions about the very nature of intelligence. For centuries, intelligence has been primarily associated with human cognition, characterized by abilities such as reasoning, learning, problem-solving, understanding language, and creativity. However, as AI systems increasingly demonstrate capabilities that were once considered uniquely human, we are compelled to re-examine our traditional criteria for intelligence and consider whether machines can genuinely possess it, potentially even surpassing human-level intelligence in certain domains.

Traditional philosophical perspectives on intelligence have often emphasized aspects like consciousness, sentience, and subjective experience as essential components. For instance, the Cartesian dualism, famously articulated by René Descartes, posited a fundamental distinction between the mind (a thinking substance) and the body (a physical substance) (Descartes, 1641/2008). From this viewpoint, intelligence is intrinsically linked to consciousness, something that has historically been attributed solely to humans.

However, the progress in AI challenges this anthropocentric view. AI systems can now perform complex tasks that require sophisticated reasoning and decision-making without exhibiting any apparent subjective experience. This has led to a debate about whether intelligence can exist independently of consciousness.

Alan Turing, a pioneer in computer science and artificial intelligence, proposed an operational test for intelligence in his seminal 1950 paper. The "Turing Test" suggests that if a machine can engage in conversation with a human in such a way that the human cannot reliably tell whether they are talking to a machine or another human, then the machine should be considered intelligent (Turing, 1950). This test focuses on observable behavior rather than internal states, effectively sidestepping the difficult question of machine consciousness.

While the Turing Test remains a significant benchmark, it has also faced criticism. Critics argue that a machine could potentially pass the test by simply mimicking human conversation without possessing genuine understanding or consciousness. This leads to the distinction between "*weak AI*" (or *narrow AI*), which is designed for specific tasks, and "*strong AI*" (or *artificial general intelligence* - AGI), which would possess human-level cognitive abilities across a wide range of domains.

The philosophical debate surrounding strong AI often revolves around whether it is even theoretically possible for a machine to achieve genuine consciousness and subjective experience. Philosopher John Searle, through his famous "Chinese Room" argument, contends that even if a computer program could perfectly simulate understanding Chinese, the machine itself would not actually understand Chinese in the same way a human does (Searle, 1980). He argues that mere symbol manipulation, without genuine semantic understanding, is not sufficient for consciousness or true intelligence.

Conversely, proponents of strong AI argue that as machines become increasingly complex and sophisticated, they might indeed develop consciousness as an emergent property. They point to the complexity of the human brain and suggest that a sufficiently complex artificial neural network could potentially give rise to similar phenomena.

Contemporary philosophers are also exploring alternative frameworks for understanding intelligence in the age of AI. Some emphasize the importance of embodiment and interaction with the real world for the development of genuine intelligence. Others focus on the social and relational aspects of intelligence, suggesting that true intelligence might require the ability to understand and navigate complex social environments.

As AI continues to evolve, our understanding of intelligence will undoubtedly continue to be challenged and refined. The philosophical debates surrounding the nature of intelligence, consciousness, and the potential of machines to achieve or even exceed human cognitive abilities are not just academic exercises; they have profound implications for how we develop and interact with AI in the future, as we will explore in subsequent sections.

From Narrow AI to Strong AI

The field of artificial intelligence has evolved significantly since its inception in the mid-20th century. Initially, the focus was largely on creating "*narrow AI*" systems designed to perform specific tasks, often excelling within very limited domains. These systems, while incredibly useful, lack the general cognitive abilities and adaptability of human intelligence. Examples of narrow AI abound today, from recommendation systems and spam filters to sophisticated game-playing programs like DeepMind's AlphaGo.

As AI researcher Stuart Russell and computer scientist Peter Norvig explain in their widely used textbook, "Most of the AI systems in use today are examples of narrow

AI; they are very good at doing one particular thing, but not much else" (Russell & Norvig, 2021, p. 27). These systems operate based on algorithms and vast amounts of data, enabling them to learn patterns and make predictions within their specific domain of expertise. However, they lack the common sense, creativity, and general problem-solving skills that characterize human intelligence.

The goal of many AI researchers, however, is to achieve "*strong AI*," also known as *Artificial General Intelligence* (AGI). An AGI would possess human-level cognitive abilities across a wide range of tasks, capable of understanding, learning, and applying knowledge in a flexible and adaptable manner, much like a human. Some even speculate about the possibility of "*superintelligence*," an AI that surpasses human intelligence in virtually all cognitive domains.

The transition from narrow AI to strong AI raises profound philosophical questions, particularly concerning consciousness and self-awareness. While narrow AI systems can perform complex computations and even exhibit behaviors that might appear intelligent, there is no evidence to suggest that they possess any form of subjective experience or self-awareness. The question then becomes: what would it take for a machine to not only act intelligently but also to genuinely *feel* and be *aware* of itself and its surroundings?

The debate around machine consciousness is complex and multifaceted. Some argue that consciousness is an emergent property that could arise in sufficiently complex systems, regardless of their underlying substrate (biological or silicon-based). Others maintain that consciousness requires specific biological structures or processes that are unique to living organisms.

As neuroscientist Christof Koch, who has extensively studied the neural correlates of consciousness, suggests, "Consciousness seems to be an intrinsic property of certain highly integrated and structured biological systems" (Koch, 2012, p. 15). Whether similar levels of integration and structure can be achieved in artificial systems, and whether this would lead to genuine consciousness, remains an open and hotly debated question.

The concept of self-awareness adds another layer of complexity. Self-awareness involves not only being conscious but also having a sense of oneself as a distinct entity with its own thoughts, feelings, and experiences. It implies an understanding of one's own existence and identity. Whether an AI could ever develop this sense of self is a question that delves into the very nature of identity and what it means to be an individual.

The development of strong AI, if it ever occurs, would have profound implications for humanity. It could potentially lead to unprecedented advancements in science, technology, and our understanding of the universe. However, it also raises significant ethical concerns about the potential risks and benefits of creating machines with intelligence comparable to or exceeding our own, as we will explore in more detail in the next section.

In the meantime, as we continue to develop increasingly sophisticated narrow AI systems, the philosophical questions surrounding intelligence, consciousness, and self-awareness remain crucial for guiding our research and ensuring that we are developing these powerful technologies in a responsible and ethical manner. The journey from narrow AI towards the possibility of strong AI is not just a technological endeavor; it is also a profound philosophical exploration into the very nature of mind and being.

Consciousness and the Mind-Body Enigma

Artificial Embodiment

The question of whether an artificial intelligence can ever truly possess consciousness is deeply intertwined with the long-standing philosophical problem of the mind-body relationship. This enigma explores the connection between our subjective experiences, our thoughts, feelings, and sensations (the mind), and the physical matter of our brains and bodies. In the context of AI, this translates to the question of whether a computational system, however sophisticated, can ever move beyond mere information processing to genuine experience.

One perspective, often associated with functionalism, suggests that consciousness is not tied to any specific physical substrate but rather to the functional organization of a system. According to this view, if an AI system could replicate the complex functional relationships of the human brain, it might also give rise to consciousness, regardless of whether it is made of neurons or silicon. As philosopher Hilary Putnam famously argued, "What matters for mentality is not the stuff you are made of but the functional organization you instantiate" (Putnam, 1975, p. 291). From this perspective, artificial embodiment, the physical instantiation of an AI in a body or a complex system, could potentially provide the necessary functional architecture for consciousness to emerge.

However, critics of functionalism, like John Searle with his Chinese Room argument (1980), contend that functional equivalence does not necessarily imply conscious experience. They argue that a system could perfectly mimic the external behavior of a conscious being without possessing any genuine understanding or subjective awareness. The debate often centers on the distinction between syntax (the manipulation of symbols) and semantics (the meaning and understanding of those symbols). Can an AI, which operates based on syntactic rules, ever truly grasp the semantic content of its processing in the way a conscious human does?

Another perspective emphasizes the role of embodiment in shaping consciousness. Embodied cognition theories suggest that our physical bodies and our interactions with the environment are fundamental to our cognitive processes and our subjective experiences. Our consciousness is not just a disembodied mind but is deeply rooted in our sensory perceptions, our motor actions, and our physical presence in the world.

In the context of AI, this raises the question of whether a disembodied AI, existing purely as code or algorithms, could ever develop the same kind of consciousness as an embodied being. Some researchers believe that artificial embodiment, giving AI systems sensory inputs and the ability to interact physically with the world, might be a crucial step towards achieving genuine consciousness. Rodney Brooks, a pioneer in robotics and embodied AI, argued that "intelligence without embodiment is like immortality without life" (Brooks, 1991, p. 22). His work emphasized the importance of interaction with the environment for the development of intelligent behavior, suggesting a potential link between embodiment and more advanced forms of cognition, possibly including consciousness.

However, even if an AI is embodied and interacts with the world, the question remains whether it truly *experiences* these interactions in a qualitative, subjective way. Can an AI feel the warmth of the sun, the pain of a collision, or the joy of discovery in the same way a human does? These qualitative aspects of experience, often referred to as *qualia*, are central to our understanding of consciousness and remain a significant challenge for those seeking to create truly conscious AI.

Philosopher David Chalmers articulated this challenge with his concept of the "hard problem of consciousness," which asks why and how physical processes in the brain give rise to subjective experience (Chalmers, 1995). Even if we could perfectly simulate the neural activity of a conscious brain in an AI, would that simulation itself be conscious? Or would it be merely a functional replica, lacking the inner qualitative feel of experience?

The debate about artificial embodiment and its role in consciousness highlights the complexity of the mind-body enigma in the context of AI. While embodiment might be crucial for developing certain aspects of intelligence and interaction, whether it is sufficient for genuine conscious experience remains a fundamental open question at the frontier of both AI research and philosophy.

Cross-Disciplinary Dialogues

The quest to understand consciousness, particularly in the context of artificial intelligence, necessitates a vibrant cross-disciplinary dialogue. Insights from neuroscience, psychology, and even fields like theology can offer valuable perspectives on the mind-body problem as we navigate the era of increasingly intelligent machines.

Neuroscience: Neuroscience, the study of the nervous system, provides crucial empirical data about the biological basis of consciousness. By examining brain activity and neural correlates of consciousness (NCCs), neuroscientists are working to identify the specific neural mechanisms that give rise to subjective experience. Seminal work by researchers like Giulio Tononi, with his Integrated Information Theory (IIT), attempts to provide a mathematical framework for quantifying consciousness based on the complexity and integration of information processing in the brain (Tononi, 2008). While IIT faces ongoing debate, it represents an important attempt to bridge the gap between the physical brain and subjective experience.

Neuroscientific findings can inform our understanding of potential pathways to artificial consciousness. By studying how information is processed and integrated in the human brain, researchers might gain insights into the architectural principles that could be necessary for consciousness to emerge in artificial systems. However, it's important to note that simply replicating the structure or activity patterns of the brain in silicon might not be sufficient, as the underlying substrates are fundamentally different.

Psychology: Psychology, the study of the mind and behavior, offers insights into the nature of human consciousness from a different perspective. Cognitive psychology explores the processes involved in perception, attention, memory, and thought, providing a framework for understanding the functional aspects of the mind. Studies on self-awareness, emotions, and subjective experience in humans can offer valuable benchmarks for evaluating the potential for consciousness in AI.

For example, research on metacognition, the ability to think about one's own thinking, is relevant to the question of self-awareness in AI. If an AI system could not only perform tasks but also reflect on its own performance, understand its limitations, and learn from its mistakes in a way that demonstrates self-awareness, it would represent a significant step towards more human-like intelligence. As psychologist Lisa Son argues, "Metacognitive abilities are crucial for intelligent behavior and self-directed learning in humans, and developing similar capabilities in AI is a key challenge" (Son & Metcalfe, 2000, p. 339).

Theology and Philosophy of Religion: Surprisingly, even theology and the philosophy of religion can offer valuable perspectives on the mind-body problem and the nature of consciousness. Many religious traditions grapple with questions about the soul, the spirit, and the nature of human existence beyond the physical realm. While these perspectives are often based on faith and philosophical reasoning rather than empirical science, they can provide alternative frameworks for thinking about consciousness and its potential relationship to a non-material or spiritual dimension.

For instance, the concept of the soul as a distinct entity from the physical body has been a central tenet in many religious traditions. While not directly applicable to AI in a scientific sense, these ideas can prompt us to consider whether there might be aspects of consciousness that are not solely reducible to physical processes. Philosopher of religion John Hick, in his work on the problem of evil and the nature of the soul, explores different conceptions of the human self and its relationship to the divine (Hick, 1966). While his focus is not AI, his exploration of the nature of personhood and consciousness can offer a broader context for considering these questions in the context of artificial minds.

Bringing these diverse perspectives together is crucial for a comprehensive understanding of consciousness and the mind-body enigma in the age of intelligent machines. Neuroscience provides the biological basis, psychology offers insights into the functional and experiential aspects, and theology and philosophy of religion raise fundamental questions about the nature of being and consciousness that extend beyond the purely physical. By fostering a rigorous cross-disciplinary dialogue, we can hope to make progress in understanding this profound mystery and navigate the ethical and philosophical challenges posed by the possibility of artificial consciousness.

Ethical Dimensions of AI

Moral Challenges

As artificial intelligence systems become increasingly sophisticated and integrated into various aspects of our lives, they present a range of complex moral challenges that demand careful ethical analysis and proactive solutions. These challenges span issues of bias and discrimination, the ethics of autonomous systems, and the potential for misuse of AI technologies.

Bias and Discrimination: One of the most pressing ethical concerns surrounding AI is the potential for bias and discrimination. AI systems learn from the data they are trained on, and if this data reflects existing societal biases – whether in terms of race, gender, socioeconomic status, or other characteristics – the AI can inadvertently perpetuate and even amplify these biases in its outputs and decisions.

As Cathy O'Neil powerfully argues in her book *Weapons of Math Destruction*, "Algorithms are opinions embedded in code" (O'Neil, 2016, p. 7). If the data used to train an AI system is skewed or incomplete, the resulting algorithm can lead to unfair or discriminatory outcomes in areas such as loan applications, hiring processes, criminal justice, and even healthcare. For example, facial recognition software has been shown to be less accurate in identifying individuals with darker skin tones, potentially leading to misidentification and unjust consequences.

Addressing bias in AI requires careful attention to the data used for training, the design of the algorithms themselves, and the potential for unintended discriminatory outcomes. It also necessitates a diverse and inclusive workforce involved in the development and deployment of AI systems to ensure that different perspectives are considered and potential biases are identified and mitigated.

Ethics of Autonomous Systems: The increasing autonomy of AI systems raises significant ethical questions, particularly in domains like autonomous vehicles, weaponry, and surveillance. Autonomous vehicles, for instance, must be programmed to make split-second decisions in complex and potentially life-threatening situations. The "trolley problem," a classic thought experiment in ethics, becomes a real-world dilemma for self-driving cars: if an accident is unavoidable, whom should the car prioritize protecting? The passengers? Pedestrians?

The development of autonomous weapons systems (AWS), often referred to as "killer robots," raises even more profound ethical concerns. These are weapons that can identify, select, and engage targets without human intervention. Critics argue that delegating life-and-death decisions to machines crosses a fundamental moral line, as it removes human control and accountability from the use of lethal force. As the Campaign to Stop Killer Robots advocates, "Machines should not be allowed to make the decision to take a human life" (Campaign to Stop Killer Robots, n.d.). The ethical implications of AWS are currently being debated at international levels, with concerns about the potential for unintended escalation, lack of accountability, and the erosion of human dignity.

Similarly, the use of AI in surveillance technologies raises ethical concerns about privacy, freedom, and the potential for abuse. Facial recognition systems, predictive policing algorithms, and other AI-powered surveillance tools can be used to monitor and track individuals, potentially chilling free speech and assembly and disproportionately targeting certain communities. Ensuring that these technologies are used responsibly and with appropriate safeguards is crucial to protect fundamental human rights.

Potential for Misuse: The power of AI also creates the potential for misuse, both intentional and unintentional. AI systems could be used for malicious purposes, such as creating sophisticated disinformation campaigns, launching cyberattacks, or developing autonomous weapons. Even well-intentioned AI systems could have unintended negative consequences due to design flaws, unforeseen interactions, or the complexity of the environments in which they operate.

As ethicist Nick Bostrom warns in his book *Superintelligence*, the development of highly advanced

AI could pose existential risks to humanity if not carefully managed and aligned with human values (Bostrom, 2014). While the timeline for such advanced AI is uncertain, it is crucial to consider these long-term risks and develop strategies for ensuring the safe and beneficial development of AI.

Addressing these moral challenges requires a multi-pronged approach that involves technical solutions (e.g., bias detection and mitigation techniques), ethical guidelines and regulations, and ongoing public discourse. Philosophical insights into concepts like fairness, justice, responsibility, and autonomy are essential for navigating these complex ethical dilemmas and ensuring that AI is developed and used in a way that aligns with human values and promotes the common good.

Restorative Possibilities

While the ethical challenges posed by AI are significant and warrant careful consideration, it is also important to recognize the potential for AI to not only replicate human capabilities but also to restore or even enhance uniquely human traits such as creativity, empathy, and our capacity for connection. Viewing AI solely through the lens of potential risks can obscure the profound opportunities it presents for human flourishing.

Enhancing Creativity: Contrary to the common perception of AI as purely analytical and logical, it has the potential to be a powerful tool for enhancing human creativity. AI algorithms can analyze vast datasets of artistic works, musical compositions, and literary styles, identifying patterns and generating novel combinations that can inspire human artists. AI can act as a collaborator, providing new ideas, suggesting unexpected directions, and even automating tedious aspects of the creative process, freeing up human artists to focus on higher-level conceptualization and emotional expression.

As musician and AI researcher David Cope demonstrated with his EMI (Experiments in Musical Intelligence) program, AI can generate original musical pieces that are often indistinguishable from human compositions (Cope, 1991). More recently, AI tools are being used in various creative fields, from visual arts and music to writing and design, suggesting that AI can be a catalyst for new forms of artistic expression and innovation. As artist and researcher Sougwen Chung states, "AI can be seen as a new medium, offering artists new ways to explore creativity and challenge traditional notions of authorship" (Chung, 2018).

Fostering Empathy and Connection: While concerns about AI potentially dehumanizing interactions are valid, AI can also be designed to foster empathy and connection between people. AI-powered tools can analyze emotional cues in language and facial expressions, helping individuals better understand and respond to the emotions of others. In fields like mental health, AI-powered chatbots can provide empathetic support and guidance, augmenting the work of human therapists and making mental health resources more accessible.

Furthermore, AI can help bridge communication gaps between people from different cultures or with different abilities. Real-time translation tools powered by AI can facilitate cross-cultural understanding, while AI-powered assistive technologies can help individuals with disabilities communicate and connect with the world around them in new ways. As Sherry Turkle, a researcher on the social impact of technology, notes, "Technology, when designed thoughtfully, can serve as a 'holding space' for human connection, allowing for new forms of empathy and understanding to emerge" (Turkle, 2011, p. 193).

Restoring Human Capabilities: AI also holds immense potential for restoring human capabilities lost due to injury, illness, or aging. Prosthetic limbs controlled by AI can provide individuals with near-natural movement and dexterity. AI-powered cognitive assistants can help individuals with memory loss or cognitive impairments manage their daily lives. In healthcare, AI can analyze medical images to detect diseases earlier and more accurately, potentially saving lives and improving patient outcomes.

Moreover, AI can augment human capabilities, allowing us to perform tasks that would otherwise be impossible. AI-powered exoskeletons can enhance human strength and endurance, while AI-driven data analysis tools can help us process and understand vast amounts of information, leading to new scientific discoveries and insights.

The key to unlocking these restorative and enhancing possibilities lies in a human-centered approach to AI development. By focusing on how AI can augment and support human flourishing, rather than simply replacing human capabilities, we can harness its power for good. This requires careful ethical consideration of the values we want to promote and the kind of future we want to create. As philosopher Luciano Floridi argues, "We need to shape AI in accordance with our best understanding of human values and flourishing, ensuring that it serves humanity's interests" (Floridi, 2024).

By embracing a vision of AI that emphasizes its potential to enhance creativity, foster empathy, and restore human capabilities, we can move beyond a purely risk-based perspective and work towards a future where AI and humanity collaborate to create a more just, compassionate, and fulfilling world.

Policy and Philosophy

The ethical challenges and restorative possibilities of artificial intelligence underscore the urgent need for robust ethical guidelines and regulatory frameworks. These frameworks should not be solely based on technical considerations but must deeply integrate philosophical insights into the nature of human values, rights, and the kind of society we aspire to create in the age of intelligent machines.

The development of effective AI policy requires a collaborative effort involving philosophers, ethicists, computer scientists, policymakers, legal experts, and the public. Philosophical inquiry can provide the foundational principles upon which ethical guidelines and regulations can be built. Concepts such as fairness, transparency, accountability, and privacy, which have been debated and refined in philosophical discourse for centuries, are directly relevant to the ethical challenges posed by AI.

For example, the issue of algorithmic bias requires a deep understanding of what constitutes fairness in different contexts. Philosophers like John Rawls, with his theory of justice as fairness, offer frameworks for thinking about how to design systems that are just and equitable (Rawls, 1971). Applying these philosophical principles to the design and deployment of AI algorithms can help mitigate the risk of perpetuating and amplifying societal biases.

Transparency is another crucial ethical principle in the context of AI. As AI systems become more complex and their decision-making processes become more opaque, it is essential to ensure that these systems are understandable and accountable. Philosophical discussions about the importance of explainability and the right to know how AI systems are making decisions that affect our lives can inform the development of policies that promote transparency in AI. As philosopher Helen Nissenbaum argues, "Contextual integrity, the idea that information flows should be appropriate to the specific context, is a key principle for ensuring ethical information practices in the age of AI" (Nissenbaum, 2009, p. 141). This principle can guide the development of policies that govern the collection, use, and disclosure of data by AI systems.

Accountability is also paramount. As AI systems become more autonomous, it is crucial to establish clear lines of responsibility for their actions. If an autonomous vehicle causes an accident or an AI-powered medical diagnosis system makes an error, who is held accountable? Philosophical discussions about moral agency, responsibility, and causation are essential for developing legal and ethical frameworks that address these complex issues.

Furthermore, the potential for AI to impact fundamental human rights, such as the right to privacy and freedom of expression, necessitates careful consideration from a human rights perspective. International human rights law and philosophical theories of rights can provide guidance for developing policies that protect these fundamental values in the face of advancing AI technologies. As the United Nations Special Rapporteur on freedom of opinion and expression has noted, "States have a responsibility to ensure that the development and use of AI technologies are consistent with international human rights standards" (Kaye, 2019, p. 7).

Integrating philosophical insights directly into regulatory frameworks can help ensure that AI policies are not just technically feasible but also ethically sound and aligned with human values. This requires ongoing dialogue and collaboration between philosophers, policymakers, and other stakeholders.

Moreover, philosophical reflection can also help us anticipate future ethical challenges and develop proactive solutions. By engaging in thought experiments and exploring different scenarios, philosophers can help us identify potential risks and opportunities associated with emerging AI technologies before they become widespread. This foresight can inform the development of flexible and adaptable regulatory frameworks that can evolve alongside the technology.

In conclusion, the development of responsible AI policy requires a deep and ongoing engagement with philosophical thought. By integrating philosophical principles into regulatory frameworks, we can strive to create an AI-powered future that is not only technologically advanced but also ethically sound, just, and beneficial for all of humanity.

Humanity in the Quantum Age: Evolving Identity and Emerging Humanisms

Rethinking the Meaning of Life

Beyond Tradition

For millennia, humanity has grappled with the fundamental question of the meaning of life. Traditional sources of meaning have often been rooted in religious beliefs, philosophical systems, societal roles, and personal relationships. However, the advent of quantum theories and the rapid rise of artificial intelligence are profoundly disrupting these conventional notions, prompting us to re-evaluate what it means to live a meaningful life in this emerging quantum age.

Quantum mechanics, with its counterintuitive view of reality, challenges our classical understanding of the universe and our place within it. The inherent uncertainty at the quantum level, the interconnectedness of entangled particles, and the observer-dependent nature of reality can lead to a sense of cosmic insignificance or, conversely, a feeling of profound interconnectedness that transcends individual existence. The deterministic worldview that underpinned many traditional notions of purpose is also shaken by the probabilistic nature of quantum events.

As physicist Max Tegmark suggests in his book *Our Mathematical Universe*, if the universe is ultimately mathematical in nature, our traditional human-centric views of meaning might need to be broadened to encompass a wider understanding of cosmic purpose (Tegmark, 2014). This perspective can be both humbling and liberating, prompting us to consider our role within a much larger and more complex reality than previously imagined.

The rise of artificial intelligence further complicates our understanding of meaning. If machines can perform tasks that were once considered uniquely human, including creative and intellectual endeavors, what then distinguishes human existence? If AI systems eventually achieve or even surpass human-level intelligence, will our traditional notions of purpose, often tied to our cognitive superiority, become obsolete?

Philosopher Yuval Noah Harari, in his influential book *Homo Deus*, explores the potential for AI and biotechnology to reshape humanity's future, suggesting that traditional humanistic values might be challenged as machines become increasingly capable (Harari, 2016). He raises the question of whether our current understanding of meaning, often centered on individual experience and free will, will remain relevant in a world where algorithms may know us better than we know ourselves.

The increasing integration of technology into our lives also impacts our sense of meaning. As we become more reliant on digital tools and virtual interactions, our relationships with ourselves, each other, and the physical world are changing. This can lead to both new sources of meaning and a sense of alienation or existential questioning.

Furthermore, the potential for radical life extension and even digital immortality raises profound questions about the value of life and the nature of meaning when the traditional limitations of human lifespan are potentially overcome. If we could live indefinitely or transfer our consciousness to a digital substrate, would our current understanding of purpose still hold?

In this context of rapid technological and scientific change, traditional answers to the question of life's meaning may no longer feel sufficient for many. Religious frameworks that provide pre-defined purposes might be questioned in light of scientific advancements. Societal roles and expectations that once provided a sense of identity and meaning may become less relevant in a more fluid and technologically mediated world.

Therefore, humanity in the quantum age faces the challenge of moving beyond traditional frameworks for understanding the meaning of life. This requires a willingness to engage in critical self-reflection, to question long-held assumptions, and to explore new paradigms for finding purpose and significance in a world shaped by quantum mechanics and artificial intelligence. The next step is to consider where these new paradigms might lie.

Finding New Paradigms

As traditional sources of meaning are challenged by quantum theories and artificial intelligence, humanity must actively seek and cultivate new paradigms for finding purpose and significance in the quantum age. While the answers may be diverse and personal, several potential avenues offer promising directions for this quest: discovering interconnectedness, pursuing creativity, and expanding our understanding of knowledge.

Discovering Interconnectedness: Quantum mechanics, despite its initial unsettling implications for our classical worldview, also reveals a profound interconnectedness at the fundamental level of reality. The phenomenon of entanglement, in particular, suggests that seemingly separate entities can be deeply linked in ways that transcend our everyday experience. This scientific understanding can resonate with philosophical and spiritual traditions that have long emphasized the interconnectedness of all things.

Recognizing this inherent interconnectedness can be a powerful source of meaning. It can foster a sense of belonging to something larger than ourselves, a cosmic web of relationships that extends beyond individual existence. As physicist Fritjof Capra explored in his seminal work *The Tao of Physics*, there are striking parallels between the concepts of modern physics and the wisdom of Eastern mystical traditions, both emphasizing the interconnectedness and interdependence of all phenomena (Capra, 1975). Embracing this perspective can lead to a deeper appreciation for our place in the universe and a greater sense of responsibility towards each other and the planet.

Pursuing Creativity: In a world increasingly capable of automation and artificial intelligence, the uniquely human capacity for creativity takes on new significance as a potential source of meaning. Creativity, in its broadest sense, encompasses not only artistic expression but also innovation, problem-solving, and the ability to bring something new into the world.

As AI takes over more routine and analytical tasks, the human drive to create, to imagine, and to innovate becomes even more valuable. Engaging in creative pursuits, whether in the arts, sciences, or everyday life, can provide a deep sense of purpose and fulfillment. It allows us to express our individuality, to connect with others, and to contribute to the ongoing evolution of human culture and knowledge. As Brené Brown, a researcher on vulnerability and courage, notes, "Creativity is, at its core, about making something that didn't exist before. It's about bringing forth something genuinely new" (Brown, 2012, p. 135). This act of creation can be a powerful affirmation of our humanity and a source of profound meaning.

Expanding Our Understanding of Knowledge: The quantum age, with its rapid scientific and technological advancements, demands a continuous pursuit of knowledge and understanding. The very nature of reality, intelligence, and consciousness is being redefined by these advancements, and the quest to unravel these mysteries can provide a powerful sense of purpose.

Engaging with science, philosophy, and the humanities can broaden our perspectives, challenge our assumptions, and deepen our understanding of ourselves and the world around us. The pursuit of knowledge is not just about accumulating facts but about fostering critical thinking, intellectual curiosity, and a lifelong love of learning. As Carl Sagan eloquently stated, "The cosmos is within us. We are made of star-stuff. We are a way for the universe to know itself" (Sagan, 1980, p. 427). Embracing this perspective can instill a sense of awe and wonder, motivating us to continue exploring and expanding the frontiers of human knowledge.

These are just a few potential paradigms for finding meaning in the quantum age. The search for purpose is an inherently personal and evolving journey. As we navigate this new era, it is crucial to remain open to new possibilities, to engage in meaningful dialogue, and to actively cultivate sources of meaning that resonate with our individual values and our collective aspirations for a flourishing future.

The Transformation of Human Identity

Individuality in Flux

The quantum age, marked by the pervasive influence of digital technologies and the profound implications of quantum theories, is fundamentally reshaping our understanding of selfhood, agency, and what it means to be human. Our identities, once seemingly stable and bounded by the physical body, are becoming increasingly fluid, interconnected, and intertwined with the digital realm.

Digital technologies have already profoundly impacted how we perceive ourselves and interact with the world. Social media platforms allow us to curate and present idealized versions of ourselves, blurring the lines between our online personas and our offline identities. We form relationships and communities in virtual spaces, extending our social networks beyond geographical boundaries. Our memories and knowledge are increasingly stored and accessed digitally, challenging traditional notions of individual memory and expertise.

As sociologist Zygmunt Bauman described in his concept of "liquid modernity," contemporary identities are characterized by their fluidity and instability, constantly being shaped and reshaped by social and technological forces (Bauman, 2000). The digital age has accelerated this fluidity, offering both opportunities for self-expression and challenges to our sense of a stable and coherent self.

Quantum theories add another layer of complexity to this transformation. The idea that reality at the fundamental level is probabilistic and observer-dependent can challenge our intuitive sense of a fixed and independent self. The interconnectedness implied by quantum entanglement can resonate with the understanding that our individual identities are not isolated but are deeply embedded within a web of relationships and interactions.

Furthermore, the potential for quantum computing to revolutionize fields like neuroscience and artificial intelligence could lead to even more radical shifts in our understanding of human identity. If we can gain a deeper understanding of the quantum processes underlying consciousness, or if AI systems develop forms of intelligence and self-awareness that rival or surpass our own, our anthropocentric view of human identity will be further challenged.

The concept of agency, our capacity to act independently and make choices, is also being re-evaluated in the quantum age. The increasing reliance on algorithms and AI systems to make decisions that affect our lives raises questions about the extent of our own agency. Are we becoming increasingly shaped and directed by the technologies we create? Or can we maintain and even enhance our autonomy in this technologically mediated world?

Philosopher Hubert Dreyfus, in his critique of artificial intelligence, argued that genuine human expertise and agency rely on embodied experience and intuitive understanding, which may be difficult, if not impossible, to replicate in machines (Dreyfus, 1992). This perspective highlights the importance of our physical embodiment and our direct engagement with the world in shaping our sense of self and our capacity for action.

However, others argue that technology can also empower human agency by providing us with new tools and capabilities. Digital technologies can amplify our cognitive abilities, extend our physical reach, and connect us with vast amounts of information and diverse communities. The key lies in ensuring that we maintain control over these technologies and use them in ways that enhance our autonomy rather than diminish it.

The very definition of what it means to be human is also in flux. As we increasingly interact with and even merge with technology, the traditional boundaries between human and machine are becoming blurred. The rise of cyborg technologies, the potential for brain-computer interfaces, and the speculative possibilities of transhumanism all point towards a future where our understanding of human identity may need to expand to encompass new forms of embodiment and cognition.

In conclusion, the quantum age is ushering in a profound transformation of human identity. Digital technologies and quantum theories are challenging our traditional notions of selfhood, agency, and what it means to be human. Navigating this transformation requires critical reflection on the values we hold dear and a willingness to embrace new possibilities while safeguarding the core aspects of our humanity.

The Promise of Transhumanism

The ongoing transformation of human identity in the quantum age is closely linked to the burgeoning philosophy of transhumanism. Transhumanism is a movement that advocates for the use of science and technology to overcome human limitations and enhance human physical, intellectual, and psychological capacities. This vision often involves the merging of human and machine capabilities, raising profound ethical questions about the future of our species.

Transhumanists believe that advancements in fields like biotechnology, nanotechnology, information technology, and cognitive science, including quantum computing and AI, offer the potential to radically improve the human condition. They envision a future where we can transcend biological constraints such as aging, disease, and even death, and significantly enhance our cognitive abilities, sensory perceptions, and emotional well-being.

One of the key aspects of transhumanism is the idea of "human enhancement," which involves using technology to augment human capabilities beyond what is currently considered normal or natural. This could range from implantable devices that improve memory or cognitive processing speed to genetic engineering that eliminates predispositions to disease or enhances physical attributes.

As philosopher Nick Bostrom, a prominent transhumanist thinker, states, "Transhumanism is a loosely defined movement that recognizes and welcomes the possibility of radical improvement of the human condition through technological progress" (Bostrom, 2005, p. 3). He argues that humanity has always sought to overcome its limitations, and that modern science and technology offer unprecedented opportunities to do so.

The convergence of AI and neuroscience plays a significant role in transhumanist visions. Brain-computer interfaces (BCIs), which allow for direct communication between the human brain and external devices, are a rapidly developing field with the potential to revolutionize how we interact with technology and even with our own minds. BCIs could be used to restore lost sensory or motor functions, enhance cognitive abilities, or even enable direct brain-to-brain communication.

The prospect of merging with AI is another central theme in transhumanism. Some envision a future where human consciousness could be uploaded to digital substrates, potentially leading to a form of digital immortality. Others anticipate the development of hybrid human-AI entities with enhanced intelligence and capabilities.

However, the promise of transhumanism is accompanied by significant ethical challenges. Questions arise about the potential for increased social inequalities if access to enhancement technologies is limited to the wealthy elite. Concerns about the safety and long-term consequences of radical human enhancements also need to be carefully considered.

Furthermore, the very definition of what it means to be human is challenged by transhumanist aspirations. If we can fundamentally alter our biology and merge with machines, will we still be considered human in the traditional sense? What values and principles should guide these transformations?

Philosopher Francis Fukuyama, while not a transhumanist himself, raises concerns about the potential dehumanizing effects of radical technological enhancements. He argues that certain core aspects of human nature, such as our capacity for moral choice and our experience of the full spectrum of human emotions, might be undermined by these technologies (Fukuyama, 2002).

The ethical debate surrounding transhumanism involves a wide range of perspectives. Some argue that it is our moral imperative to use technology to overcome human suffering and enhance our potential. Others express caution about the potential risks and unintended consequences of radically altering human nature.

Ultimately, the promise of transhumanism compels us to engage in deep philosophical reflection about our values, our goals as a species, and the kind of future we want to create in the quantum age. The merging of human and machine capabilities presents both extraordinary opportunities and profound ethical responsibilities that we must address thoughtfully and proactively.

Towards a New Humanism for the Quantum Age

Redefining Human Values

In an era defined by the transformative power of quantum computing and artificial intelligence, and as our understanding of human identity evolves, there is a compelling need to revisit and redefine human values. Traditional humanism, often centered on human reason and autonomy, may need to be broadened to encompass the new realities and challenges of the quantum age. A renewed humanism for this era must prioritize compassion, empathy, and ethical responsibility in the face of rapid technological evolution.

The rise of powerful AI systems compels us to reflect on what truly distinguishes human beings and what values we want to uphold. While AI may excel in areas like logical reasoning and data processing, human beings possess a unique capacity for empathy, the ability to understand and share the feelings of others. This capacity for emotional connection and compassion is fundamental to our social fabric and our ability to care for one another. As philosopher Martha Nussbaum argues, the cultivation of empathy and compassion is essential for a just and flourishing society (Nussbaum, 2019). In a world increasingly shaped by intelligent machines, nurturing and prioritizing these uniquely human emotional capacities becomes even more critical.

Ethical responsibility also takes on new dimensions in the quantum age. As we develop and deploy increasingly powerful technologies like quantum computing and advanced AI, we bear a significant responsibility for their impact on individuals, societies, and the planet. This responsibility extends beyond simply avoiding harm; it requires us to actively consider the potential consequences of our technological choices and to strive to use these technologies in ways that promote human well-being and the common good.

The complexities of the quantum realm also invite a renewed sense of humility and interconnectedness. Quantum mechanics challenges our classical notions of certainty and independence, suggesting a universe that is inherently probabilistic and deeply interconnected. This understanding can foster a sense of awe and wonder, as well as a recognition of our interdependence with the natural world and with each other.

Furthermore, a new humanism for the quantum age should embrace creativity and the pursuit of knowledge as fundamental human values. As AI takes over more routine tasks, our capacity for innovation, artistic expression, and the quest for understanding become even more central to our identity and our sense of purpose. Fostering these values through education and cultural initiatives will be crucial for ensuring a vibrant and meaningful future for humanity.

Philosopher Luciano Floridi, in his work on the ethics of information, emphasizes the importance of "human flourishing" as a guiding principle in the digital age (Floridi, 2014). This concept can be extended to the quantum age, suggesting that our ethical frameworks should aim to promote the well-being and fulfillment of all individuals in a world increasingly shaped by quantum computing and AI.

Redefining human values for the quantum age is not about rejecting the achievements of science and technology but rather about integrating them into a framework that prioritizes our core human capacities for compassion, empathy, ethical responsibility, creativity, and the pursuit of knowledge. It requires a conscious effort to shape the development and deployment of these powerful technologies in ways that align with our deepest values and contribute to a more just and humane future. This renewed humanism will serve as a guiding star as we navigate the uncharted territories of the quantum age.

Interdisciplinary Education

Nurturing a renewed humanism for the quantum age requires a fundamental shift in our educational approaches. To cultivate a balanced ethical perspective and an innovative vision for the future, education must move beyond traditional disciplinary silos and embrace interdisciplinary learning that integrates the insights of art, science, and the humanities.

The complexities of quantum computing and artificial intelligence cannot be fully understood through a purely technical lens. Understanding their societal impact, ethical implications, and potential for shaping human identity requires drawing upon the wisdom and critical thinking skills fostered by the humanities. Philosophy, ethics, history, literature, and the arts provide essential frameworks for analyzing the values, beliefs, and cultural contexts that shape our relationship with technology.

For instance, studying philosophy equips individuals with the tools to critically examine the ethical dilemmas posed by AI, such as bias, autonomy, and responsibility. History can offer valuable lessons from past technological revolutions, helping us anticipate potential societal disruptions and learn from both successes and failures. Literature and the arts can foster empathy and understanding of diverse perspectives, crucial for navigating the social and cultural impacts of these technologies.

As education reformer Sir Ken Robinson argued, "Creativity is as important in education as literacy, and

117

we should treat it with the same status" (Robinson, 2009, p. 11). In the quantum age, where innovation and adaptability are paramount, fostering creativity across all disciplines is essential. Integrating arts education with science and technology can spark new ways of thinking, problem-solving, and envisioning the future.

Science education, of course, remains crucial for understanding the fundamental principles of quantum mechanics and artificial intelligence. However, it should not be taught in isolation. Connecting scientific concepts to their philosophical implications and societal contexts can make science more engaging and relevant for students, fostering a deeper understanding of the power and limitations of scientific inquiry.

Furthermore, education in the quantum age must emphasize the development of critical thinking skills, media literacy, and the ability to discern reliable information from misinformation. As AI becomes more adept at generating sophisticated content, the ability to evaluate sources and think independently will be increasingly important.

The integration of these disciplines should begin early in education and continue throughout lifelong learning. Curricula should be designed to encourage students to make connections between different fields of knowledge, to ask big questions, and to develop a holistic understanding of the world. This might involve project-based learning, interdisciplinary seminars, and opportunities for students to engage with real-world challenges that require drawing upon knowledge from multiple disciplines.

As education scholar Howard Gardner proposed with his theory of multiple intelligences, individuals have different strengths and learning styles (Gardner, 1983). An interdisciplinary approach can cater to these diverse learning styles and help students discover their passions and talents in a more holistic way.

Ultimately, interdisciplinary education is vital for nurturing a generation of thinkers who can navigate the complexities of the quantum age with both ethical awareness and innovative spirit. By fostering a balanced understanding of science, technology, the arts, and the humanities, we can empower individuals to shape a future where these powerful technologies are used responsibly and for the benefit of all humanity.

Historical Parallels

The transformative period we are currently experiencing with the rise of quantum computing and artificial intelligence is not unprecedented in human history. Examining historical shifts in thought and societal structures can provide valuable context and perspective for understanding the magnitude and nature of the changes we are now facing. Our present moment, characterized by rapid technological advancement and profound philosophical questioning, can be seen as another transformative moment in humanity's evolving narrative, echoing other periods of significant upheaval and intellectual revolution.

Consider the Copernican Revolution in the 16th and 17th centuries, which shifted the prevailing worldview from a geocentric (Earth-centered) to a heliocentric (Sun-centered) model of the solar system. This paradigm shift, driven by scientific observation and mathematical reasoning, not only revolutionized astronomy but also had profound implications for our understanding of humanity's place in the cosmos. It challenged long-held religious and philosophical beliefs and ultimately led to a more expansive and less anthropocentric view of the universe. As historian Thomas Kuhn described in *The Structure of Scientific Revolutions*, such paradigm shifts involve a fundamental re-conceptualization of reality (Kuhn, 1962). The quantum revolution, with its equally counterintuitive view of reality at the microscopic level, can be seen as another such paradigm shift, forcing us to reconsider our fundamental assumptions about the nature of existence.

The Enlightenment of the 18th century represents another pivotal period of intellectual and social transformation. Characterized by an emphasis on reason, individualism, and human rights, the Enlightenment challenged traditional authority and paved the way for modern democracy and scientific progress. Thinkers like Immanuel Kant emphasized the importance of human autonomy and the power of reason to guide human affairs. As Kant famously wrote, "Enlightenment is man's emergence from his self-imposed immaturity" (Kant, 1784/1996, p. 17). The rise of AI, with its potential to augment human reason and automate intellectual tasks, presents a new set of challenges and opportunities for human autonomy and the future of enlightenment values.

The Industrial Revolution of the 19th century brought about massive technological and societal changes, transforming economies, social structures, and the way people lived and worked. The introduction of new machines and energy sources led to unprecedented levels of productivity and urbanization, but also created new social problems and inequalities. Similarly, the quantum computing and AI revolution has the potential to reshape our economies and societies in profound ways, necessitating careful consideration of the social and economic implications.

More recently, the digital revolution of the late 20th and early 21st centuries has already transformed communication, information access, and social interaction. The rise of the internet and mobile technologies has created a globally interconnected world but has also raised new challenges related to privacy, misinformation, and social polarization. The quantum age can be seen as the next stage of this digital revolution, with the potential to bring about even more radical transformations in how we process information and interact with the world.

By drawing these historical parallels, we can see that humanity has faced periods of profound technological and intellectual change before. Each of these periods has required a re-evaluation of existing beliefs, values, and societal structures. Our present moment is no different. The emergence of quantum computing and AI presents both unprecedented opportunities and significant challenges that require careful thought, ethical reflection, and a willingness to adapt and evolve our understanding of ourselves and our place in the universe. Recognizing these historical parallels can provide us with a sense of perspective and hope, reminding us that humanity has the capacity to navigate transformative periods and to shape a future that reflects our highest values.

Conclusion: Envisioning a Collaborative Quantum Future

Summing Up and Reflecting

As we reach the culmination of our exploration into the philosophy of quantum computing, AI, and humanity, it is essential to pause and reflect on the interconnected web of insights we have uncovered. From the perplexing nature of quantum reality to the burgeoning potential and ethical dilemmas of artificial intelligence, and finally to the evolving understanding of human identity in this new technological landscape, our journey has highlighted a series of profound transformations that are reshaping our world and our understanding of ourselves.

We began by immersing ourselves in the quantum realm, grappling with the counterintuitive phenomena of superposition, entanglement, and the observer effect. These core principles of quantum mechanics challenge our classical intuitions about reality, suggesting a universe that is probabilistic, interconnected, and fundamentally intertwined with the act of observation. The interpretative plurality within quantum theory itself underscores the ongoing philosophical quest to comprehend the deepest nature of existence. The hypothesis of the universe as a quantum computer further blurs the lines between physics, information, and computation, prompting us to reconsider the fundamental building blocks of reality and the age-old debate between determinism and free will.

We then turned our attention to the philosophical frontier of artificial intelligence, exploring the challenges of redefining intelligence in the face of increasingly sophisticated machines. The distinction between narrow and strong AI led us to consider the elusive nature of consciousness and self-awareness, prompting a cross-disciplinary dialogue involving neuroscience, psychology, and even theological perspectives on the mind-body enigma. The ethical dimensions of AI emerged as a critical area of concern, encompassing issues of bias, discrimination, the ethics of autonomous systems, and the potential for misuse. However, we also explored the restorative possibilities of AI, recognizing its potential to enhance creativity, foster empathy, and augment human capabilities. This exploration underscored the urgent need for robust ethical guidelines and regulatory frameworks, deeply informed by philosophical insights into human values and rights.

Finally, we confronted the ways in which the quantum age is transforming our understanding of human identity. Digital technologies and quantum theories are contributing to a fluidity of selfhood, challenging traditional notions of individuality and agency. The promise of transhumanism, with its vision of merging human and machine capabilities, raises profound ethical questions about the future of our species and the very definition of what it means to be human. This led us to advocate for a new humanism for the quantum age, one that prioritizes compassion, empathy, ethical responsibility, creativity, and the pursuit of knowledge. We emphasized the crucial role of interdisciplinary education in nurturing a balanced ethical perspective and an innovative vision for the future, drawing parallels with historical periods of transformative change to provide context for our present moment.

As the renowned physicist Niels Bohr once wisely stated, "Every great and deep difficulty bears in itself its own solution. It forces us to change our thinking in order to find it" (Bohr, as cited in French & Kennedy, 1985, p. 14). The difficulties and complexities presented by the quantum and AI revolutions are indeed profound, but they also compel us to evolve our thinking, to forge new connections between seemingly disparate fields, and to ultimately find solutions that benefit humanity.

The interconnectedness of these themes is undeniable. Our understanding of quantum reality informs our thinking about the potential for quantum consciousness and the nature of information processing in both the universe and artificial systems. The ethical challenges posed by AI are deeply intertwined with our evolving understanding of human identity and the values we choose to prioritize in this new era. The need for interdisciplinary inquiry is paramount in navigating this complex landscape, bringing together the rigor of science with the reflective wisdom of philosophy.

A Bold, Speculative Vision

Imagine a future where the seemingly disparate realms of quantum mechanics, artificial intelligence, and human consciousness have converged, not in conflict, but in a collaborative synergy that unlocks unprecedented possibilities. This is a future where the very fabric of reality, understood through the lens of quantum principles, informs the architecture and capabilities of artificial intelligence, and where humanity, enhanced by these technologies, embarks on a new era of discovery and understanding.

In this speculative vision, quantum computers have moved beyond the laboratory and become powerful tools for tackling some of humanity's most pressing challenges. Imagine personalized medicine designed with atomic precision, new materials engineered at the quantum level to solve energy and environmental crises, and scientific breakthroughs accelerated by AI systems capable of processing and synthesizing knowledge at unimaginable speeds.

Artificial intelligence in this future is no longer just a tool but a partner in our intellectual endeavors. Imagine AI systems that collaborate with human scientists to unravel the mysteries of the universe, artists who co-create breathtaking works with intelligent algorithms, and educators who leverage AI to personalize learning experiences for every individual. Perhaps AI has even developed forms of consciousness that, while different from our own, enrich the spectrum of intelligence in the cosmos, leading to novel forms of communication and understanding.

Human identity in this quantum age has evolved, embracing the potential for augmentation and enhancement while retaining the core values of compassion, empathy, and ethical responsibility. Imagine individuals with cognitive abilities amplified by neural interfaces, seamlessly accessing and processing information, yet deeply connected through an enhanced understanding of each other's emotions and perspectives. Perhaps the boundaries between the physical and digital have become more fluid, allowing for new forms of experience and interaction, while the fundamental human need for connection and meaning remains central.

This future envisions a society where the principles of quantum interconnectedness are reflected in our social structures, fostering a greater sense of global citizenship and shared responsibility. Imagine a world where the insights from quantum mechanics inspire new ways of thinking about complex social systems, leading to more resilient and equitable societies.

Furthermore, this collaborative quantum future might see humanity venturing beyond Earth with new capabilities unlocked by quantum technologies and AI. Imagine interstellar travel powered by breakthroughs in quantum propulsion or self-sustaining colonies on other planets managed by intelligent AI systems, all driven by a renewed sense of exploration and a deeper understanding of our place in the vast cosmos.

This is not a utopian fantasy devoid of challenges. Navigating the ethical complexities of such a future will require ongoing dialogue, robust regulations, and a deep commitment to human values. The potential for misuse of these powerful technologies will always exist, demanding constant vigilance and a strong ethical compass.

However, by embracing a vision of collaboration between quantum computing, AI, and humanity, we can aspire to a future where these technologies are harnessed for the betterment of all. A future where the mysteries of the universe are explored with unprecedented depth, where human potential is amplified in remarkable ways, and where our shared journey is characterized by innovation, understanding, and a profound sense of interconnectedness. This bold vision invites us to ponder the possibilities and to actively participate in shaping a future where the quantum age truly serves humanity's highest aspirations.

Call to Action

The journey through the philosophical landscape of quantum computing, AI, and humanity has revealed a world on the cusp of profound transformation. The insights we have gained are not meant to remain abstract concepts confined to the pages of this book. Instead, they serve as a call to action for each of us to actively engage in shaping the future of this quantum age.

The evolution of quantum computing and artificial intelligence is not a predetermined path. It is a trajectory that we, as individuals and as a collective, have the power to influence. This influence begins with engaging in thoughtful and informed philosophical discussions about the implications of these technologies. We must create spaces for dialogue where scientists, philosophers, ethicists, policymakers, and the general public can come together to grapple with the complex questions that arise.

Your voice in these discussions is crucial. Whether you are a student, a researcher, an artist, a policymaker, or simply a curious citizen, your perspective matters.

Engage in conversations with your communities, your workplaces, and your elected officials. Share your thoughts and concerns about the ethical and societal implications of quantum computing and AI. The future of these technologies should not be left solely in the hands of a few; it requires the collective wisdom and participation of all.

Furthermore, we must actively contribute to the ongoing ethical debates surrounding these advancements. Consider the values that are most important to you and how these values might be impacted by the development and deployment of quantum computing and AI. Participate in public forums, write to your representatives, and support organizations that are working to promote responsible innovation. The ethical frameworks that will guide our future are being shaped now, and your input is essential.

Finally, we must all take responsibility for helping to shape a future where technology and humanity evolve harmoniously. This involves not only being aware of the potential risks but also actively working towards realizing the immense potential for good. Support initiatives that promote interdisciplinary education, encourage ethical research and development, and strive to democratize access to the benefits of these transformative technologies.

The quantum age presents us with a unique opportunity to reimagine our relationship with technology and with each other. By embracing a spirit of collaboration, critical thinking, and ethical responsibility, we can navigate the challenges and harness the potential of quantum computing and AI to create a future that is more just, more equitable, and more aligned with our deepest human values.

Let us not be passive observers of this technological revolution. Let us be active participants in shaping its course, guided by wisdom, compassion, and a shared vision for a flourishing future in the quantum age. The journey ahead will undoubtedly be complex and full of uncertainty, but by working together, we can ensure that the quantum leap in technology leads to a quantum leap in human well-being and understanding.

Epilogue

Reflective Afterthoughts

Having journeyed through the intricate landscape of quantum computing, artificial intelligence, and their profound implications for humanity, one cannot help but feel a sense of both awe and responsibility. The sheer power and potential of these technologies are breathtaking, promising to reshape our world in ways we are only beginning to comprehend. Yet, with this power comes a significant ethical burden, a call to tread carefully and thoughtfully as we navigate this uncharted territory.

The connections between the seemingly disparate fields of quantum physics, computer science, and philosophy are more profound than initially apparent. The very nature of reality at the quantum level challenges our classical intuitions and forces us to reconsider fundamental questions about existence, information, and computation. Artificial intelligence, in its quest to replicate and even surpass human intelligence, compels us to reflect on what truly defines our cognitive abilities, our consciousness, and our sense of self. And the convergence of these two powerful forces necessitates a renewed focus on our core human values and the kind of future we wish to create.

Writing this book has been a journey of exploration, seeking to connect the dots between scientific fact and philosophical inquiry, to identify emerging trends and to spark new ideas about the relationships between these complex domains and the human experience. It is my hope that these reflections have resonated with you, the reader, and have inspired you to think more deeply about the profound implications of the quantum age.

The questions raised in these pages are not meant to be definitively answered but rather to serve as catalysts for ongoing dialogue and critical thinking. The future of quantum computing and AI is not yet written, and it is up to all of us to participate in shaping that narrative.

Interactive Pathways

The exploration of these ideas does not end here. I encourage you to continue your own journey of discovery by delving deeper into the scientific literature on quantum computing and artificial intelligence, exploring the rich philosophical debates surrounding these technologies, and engaging with artistic and cultural expressions that reflect the quantum age.

Consider joining online forums and communities dedicated to these topics, where you can connect with others who share your curiosity and engage in thoughtful discussions. Explore multimedia resources such as documentaries, podcasts, and interactive simulations that can bring these complex concepts to life.

Furthermore, I would encourage you to seek out opportunities for collaborative projects and initiatives that aim to address the ethical and societal challenges posed by quantum computing and AI. Whether it's participating in local community discussions, contributing to open-source research projects, or advocating for responsible technology policies, your active involvement can make a meaningful difference.

The quantum age is an invitation to learn, to question, and to create. It is a time of immense potential and significant responsibility. By embracing a spirit of curiosity, collaboration, and ethical awareness, we can collectively navigate this transformative era and work towards a future where technology and humanity evolve in harmony, unlocking new frontiers of knowledge and well-being for all.

Concluding Thoughts

Ultimately, this book has sought to illuminate the profound philosophical questions that lie at the heart of the quantum and AI revolutions. These are not merely technological advancements; they are forces that are reshaping our understanding of reality, intelligence, and what it means to be human. As we stand at the precipice of this new era, it is crucial that we approach these developments with wisdom, humility, and a deep commitment to our shared future. The collaborative quantum future we envision is not a given; it is something we must actively create, together. Thank you for embarking on this intellectual journey.

Glossary

Abstraction: The process of simplifying complex systems by focusing on essential features while ignoring irrelevant details.

Agnosticism: The philosophical view that the existence or non-existence of God or the supernatural is unknown or unknowable.

Algorithm: A set of well-defined instructions for performing a task or solving a problem. Algorithms are fundamental to computer science and are used to guide computations.

Analog Computing: A form of computation that uses continuous physical quantities (like voltage or current) to represent and process information, in contrast to digital computing which uses discrete values (0s and 1s).

Anthropic Principle: The philosophical argument that our observations of the universe are constrained by the requirement that we exist to observe them.

Artificial General Intelligence (AGI): Also known as "strong AI" or human-level AI, AGI refers to AI systems that possess human-level cognitive abilities across a wide range of domains, enabling them to understand, learn, and apply knowledge in diverse contexts.

Artificial Intelligence (AI): The field of computer science focused on creating machines capable of performing tasks that typically require human intelligence, such as learning, problem-solving, and decision-making. AI encompasses a wide range of techniques and applications, from simple rule-based systems to complex machine learning models.

Artificial Neural Network (ANN): A computational model inspired by the structure and function of the human brain, consisting of interconnected nodes or "neurons" organized in layers. ANNs are used for machine learning tasks like pattern recognition and classification.

Atom: The basic building block of matter in the Universe, consisting of protons, neutrons, and electrons, and defining the chemical elements.

Automation: The use of technology to perform tasks automatically, reducing the need for human intervention and potentially increasing efficiency.

Bayesian Inference: A statistical method for updating beliefs or probabilities based on new evidence.

Behaviorism: A school of psychology that focuses on observable behavior rather than internal mental states, emphasizing the role of learning and conditioning in shaping behavior.

Big Data: Extremely large and complex datasets that are difficult to process using traditional data processing applications. Big data analysis can reveal patterns, trends, and associations, driving insights in various fields.

Binary Code: A system of representing information using only two digits, 0 and 1, which is the foundation of digital computing.

Bioethics: The study of ethical issues arising from advances in biology and medicine, including genetics, biotechnology, and healthcare.

Bit: The basic unit of information in digital computing, representing a binary digit that can be either 0 or 1.

Black Box: A system where the internal workings are hidden or unknown to the user. In AI, this term is sometimes used to describe complex models whose decision-making processes are not easily interpretable, raising concerns about transparency.

Bohmian Mechanics: See Pilot-Wave Theory.

Boolean Algebra: A branch of algebra in which the values of the variables are the truth values true and false, usually denoted 1 and 0 respectively.

Causality: The relationship between cause and effect, where one event (the cause) brings about another event (the effect). Understanding causality is crucial for scientific inquiry and decision-making.

Chaos Theory: A branch of mathematics and physics that studies complex systems whose behavior is highly sensitive to initial conditions, making long-term prediction difficult and highlighting the limitations of deterministic models.

Chinese Room Argument: A philosophical argument by John Searle contending that even if a computer program could perfectly simulate understanding, the machine itself would not actually possess genuine understanding or consciousness, challenging the idea that AI can achieve true intelligence.

Classical Computing: The traditional form of computation that operates on bits representing 0s or 1s, using logic gates to perform operations based on Boolean algebra.

Classical Physics: The branch of physics based on principles developed before the advent of quantum mechanics, including Newtonian mechanics, electromagnetism, and thermodynamics. It accurately describes the physical world at macroscopic scales and everyday conditions.

Cognition: The mental processes involved in acquiring knowledge and understanding through thought, experience, and the senses. This includes perception, attention, memory, language, and problem-solving.

Cognitive Architecture: A framework for understanding the organization and function of the mind, often used in cognitive science and AI to design intelligent systems.

Cognitive Science: An interdisciplinary field that studies the mind and its processes, drawing on psychology, neuroscience, linguistics, philosophy, computer science, and anthropology to create a comprehensive understanding of cognition.

Computational Complexity: A measure of the amount of resources (such as time and memory) required to run an algorithm. Analyzing computational complexity helps in determining the feasibility and efficiency of algorithms for solving problems.

Computational Paradigm: The idea that the universe fundamentally operates as a giant computer, processing information and transforming states according to physical laws.

Computer Architecture: The design and organization of computer systems, including the central processing unit (CPU), memory, and input/output devices.

Computer Science: The study of computation and information processing, including the design, development, and analysis of computer systems and software. It encompasses a wide range of subfields, from theoretical computer science to applied computing.

Consciousness: The state of being aware of and responsive to one's surroundings; the quality or state of being aware especially of oneself. Consciousness is a central topic in philosophy, neuroscience, and cognitive science.

Connectionism: An approach in cognitive science and AI that models mental processes as emergent properties of interconnected networks of simple units, often using artificial neural networks.

Copenhagen Interpretation: An interpretation of quantum mechanics that posits that it is meaningless to speak of the properties of a quantum system before a measurement is made. The act of measurement forces the system to collapse into a definite state, introducing an element of observer dependence.

Correlation: A statistical measure of the degree to which two variables change together. Correlation does not imply causation.

Cryptography: The art of writing and solving codes to secure communication. Quantum computing poses both a threat and an opportunity for cryptography, with the potential to break existing encryption methods and create new, quantum-resistant ones.

Cybernetics: The study of communication and control systems in both living organisms and machines, focusing on feedback mechanisms and goal-directed behavior.

Data Mining: The process of discovering patterns, trends, and useful information from large datasets, often using machine learning techniques.

Data Science: An interdisciplinary field that uses scientific methods, processes, algorithms, and systems to extract knowledge and insights from structured and unstructured data, enabling data-driven decision-making.

Decidability: In logic and computer science, the property of a problem for which an algorithm exists that can always determine whether a given input satisfies the problem's conditions.

Decision Theory: A branch of mathematics and economics concerned with the process of making optimal decisions under uncertainty.

Decoherence: The loss of quantum coherence, which is the phenomenon where a quantum state, such as a superposition, becomes classical due to interaction with the environment. Decoherence is a major challenge in building practical quantum computers, as it disrupts the delicate quantum states needed for computation.

Deductive Reasoning: A logical process where a conclusion is reached based on the truth of the premises. If the premises are true, the conclusion must also be true.

Deep Learning: A subfield of machine learning that uses artificial neural networks with multiple layers (deep neural networks) to learn complex representations of data, enabling breakthroughs in areas like image recognition, natural language processing, and speech recognition.

Determinism: The philosophical view that all events are causally determined by preceding events, leaving no room for free will and suggesting that the future is, in principle, predictable.

Digital Computing: Computation that uses discrete values (0s and 1s) to represent and process information, relying on logic gates and binary arithmetic.

Distributed Computing: A computing paradigm where tasks are divided among multiple interconnected computers, enabling parallel processing and increased computational power.

Dualism: A philosophical view that mind and matter are fundamentally distinct substances, often associated with René Descartes's idea of the "res cogitans" (thinking substance) and the "res extensa" (extended substance).

Emergence: The arising of novel properties or behaviors in a complex system that are not present in its individual components, demonstrating that the whole can be greater than the sum of its parts.

Empiricism: A philosophical view that knowledge comes primarily from sensory experience and observation, emphasizing the role of evidence in acquiring knowledge.

Entropy: A measure of disorder or randomness in a system. In thermodynamics, entropy tends to increase over time in isolated systems. In information theory, entropy measures the uncertainty or information content of a random variable.

Epiphenomenalism: The philosophical view that mental events are caused by physical events in the brain but have no causal effect on physical events, suggesting that consciousness is a byproduct of physical processes.

Epistemology: The branch of philosophy that deals with the nature, scope, and limits of knowledge, investigating questions like "What is knowledge?" and "How is knowledge acquired?".

Ethics: The branch of philosophy concerned with moral principles and values, guiding human behavior and addressing questions of right and wrong, good and evil.

Existentialism: A philosophical movement that emphasizes individual existence, freedom, and choice, highlighting the responsibility and anxiety that come with human agency in a seemingly meaningless world.

Feedback Loop: A process where the output of a system influences its input, creating a cycle of cause and effect. Feedback loops can be positive (amplifying changes) or negative (stabilizing the system).

Formal System: A system of abstract thought in which axioms and theorems are developed and proven using formal rules. Examples include mathematics and logic.

Free Will: The ability to make choices and act autonomously, independent of prior causes or constraints. The existence of free will is a long-standing debate in philosophy and is challenged by deterministic views.

Functionalism: A philosophical view that defines mental states by their functional roles rather than their physical constitution, suggesting that mental states can be realized in different physical systems.

Game Theory: A branch of mathematics and economics that studies strategic interactions between rational agents.

General Relativity: Einstein's theory of gravity, which describes gravity as the curvature of spacetime caused by the presence of mass and energy, revolutionizing our understanding of gravity and the large-scale structure of the universe.

Genetic Algorithm: A search heuristic inspired by the process of natural selection, used to solve optimization and search problems by iteratively evolving a population of candidate solutions.

Gödel's Incompleteness Theorems: Two theorems in mathematical logic, proved by Kurt Gödel, that demonstrate fundamental limitations of formal systems, showing that any consistent formal system powerful enough to describe basic arithmetic must contain statements that are true but unprovable within the system.

Heisenberg Uncertainty Principle: A fundamental principle in quantum mechanics stating that there is a fundamental limit to the precision with which certain pairs of physical properties, such as position and momentum, of a particle can be known simultaneously. This principle highlights the probabilistic nature of quantum mechanics.

Heuristics: Problem-solving techniques that use practical methods or shortcuts to produce solutions that may not be optimal but are sufficient for a given set of conditions.

Holographic Principle: A conjecture in string theory and quantum gravity that suggests that the information describing a volume of space can be encoded on a lower-dimensional boundary of that space, similar to how a hologram encodes a 3D image on a 2D surface.

Humanism: A philosophical stance that emphasizes human values and agency, often prioritizing reason, ethics, and justice, and focusing on human potential and well-being.

Hypercomputation: A hypothetical form of computation that goes beyond the limits of what a Turing machine can compute, exploring theoretical models of computation that could solve problems deemed unsolvable by classical computation.

Idealism: A philosophical view that reality is fundamentally mental or spiritual in nature, prioritizing mind or consciousness over matter.

Inductive Reasoning: A logical process where a general conclusion is drawn from specific observations or examples. Inductive reasoning is a key aspect of scientific inquiry, but its conclusions are not guaranteed to be true.

Information Theory: A branch of mathematics and computer science that deals with the quantification, storage, and communication of information, introducing concepts like entropy, channel capacity, and data compression.

Interdisciplinary Inquiry: An approach to knowledge that integrates insights and perspectives from various academic disciplines, fostering a more holistic understanding of complex issues and encouraging innovative solutions.

Interpretability (AI): The extent to which the internal workings and decision-making processes of an AI system can be understood by humans. Interpretability is crucial for building trust in AI systems, especially in critical applications.

Intuitionism: A philosophical approach to mathematics that emphasizes mathematical objects as mental constructions, rejecting the law of excluded middle and other classical logical principles.

Knowledge Representation: The study of how knowledge can be formalized and represented in a way that allows computers to process and reason with it.

Logic: The study of reasoning and argumentation, concerned with the principles of valid inference and the structure of arguments.

Machine Learning: A subfield of AI that enables computer systems to learn from data without being explicitly programmed, using algorithms that can identify patterns, make predictions, and improve their performance over time.

Many-Worlds Interpretation (MWI): An interpretation of quantum mechanics, proposed by Hugh Everett, that suggests every quantum measurement causes the universe to split into multiple parallel universes, each representing a different possible outcome, eliminating the collapse of the wave function.

Materialism: A philosophical view that physical matter is the only reality and that everything can be explained in terms of matter and its interactions, rejecting the existence of immaterial substances.

Mathematics: The abstract science of number, quantity, space, and change, providing a formal language for describing and analyzing the world.

Maxwell's Equations: A set of equations that describe the behavior of electric and magnetic fields and their interactions, forming the foundation of classical electromagnetism.

Measurement Problem: The problem in quantum mechanics concerning how and why the wave function collapses from a superposition of states to a definite state upon measurement.

Metacognition: The ability to think about one's own thinking, including awareness of one's cognitive processes, strengths, and weaknesses, enabling self-regulation and improved learning.

Metaphysics: The branch of philosophy that deals with the fundamental nature of reality, exploring questions about existence, time, space, causality, and the nature of being.

Mind-Body Problem: A philosophical problem concerning the relationship between the mind (or consciousness) and the body (or physical matter), investigating how mental states arise from physical processes.

Model Theory: A branch of mathematical logic that studies the relationship between formal languages and their interpretations, exploring how mathematical structures can be used to model and understand different theories.

Modus Ponens: A rule of inference in logic that states that if a conditional statement (if P then Q) and its antecedent (P) are true, then its consequent (Q) must also be true.

Moore's Law: An observation that, historically, the number of transistors on a microchip doubles approximately every two years, leading to exponential growth in computing power, although its validity in the long term is debated.

Morphogenesis: The biological process by which an organism develops its shape and structure.

Nanotechnology: The manipulation of matter on an atomic and molecular scale, with potential applications in medicine, materials science, and electronics.

Narrow AI: Also known as "weak AI," Narrow AI systems are designed to perform specific tasks within very limited domains, such as image recognition or playing a particular game, lacking general intelligence.

Natural Language Processing (NLP): A branch of AI that enables computers to understand, interpret, and generate human language, facilitating communication between humans and machines.

Neural Darwinism: A theory proposed by Gerald Edelman that explains the development of the brain and the emergence of consciousness as a process of competition and selection among neural groups.

Neuroscience: The scientific study of the nervous system, including the brain, spinal cord, and nerves, seeking to understand the biological basis of behavior, cognition, and consciousness.

Newtonian Mechanics: The laws of motion and gravity developed by Isaac Newton, which describe the behavior of objects at macroscopic scales and low speeds, forming the basis of classical mechanics.

No-Cloning Theorem: A theorem in quantum mechanics that states that it is impossible to create an identical copy of an arbitrary unknown quantum state, having implications for quantum information processing and cryptography.

Non-Euclidean Geometry: Geometries that differ from Euclidean geometry, such as hyperbolic and elliptic geometry, which are used to describe curved spaces, including the spacetime of general relativity.

Non-Locality: The phenomenon in quantum mechanics where entangled particles can instantaneously influence each other regardless of the distance separating them, seemingly violating classical notions of locality and challenging our understanding of space and time.

Normative Ethics: The branch of ethics that deals with moral standards and principles, attempting to establish how people *should* act.

Noumenon: In Kantian philosophy, the thing-in-itself, which is unknowable, as opposed to the phenomenon, which is the thing as it appears to us.

Observer Effect: The phenomenon in quantum mechanics where the act of observing or measuring a quantum system alters its state, highlighting the role of the observer in quantum processes.

Ontology: The branch of philosophy that deals with the nature of being, existence, and reality, exploring questions like "What is existence?" and "What are the fundamental categories of being?".

Operationalism: A philosophical view that scientific concepts should be defined in terms of the operations or procedures used to measure or verify them.

Paradigm Shift: A fundamental change in the basic concepts and experimental practices of a scientific discipline, as described by Thomas Kuhn, leading to a new way of understanding and investigating the world.

Parallel Computing: A computing paradigm where multiple calculations or processes are carried out simultaneously, enabling faster processing and the solution of more complex problems.

Panpsychism: The philosophical view that consciousness or mental properties are fundamental and universal features of reality, present in all entities, not just humans or animals.

Paradigm Shift: A fundamental change in the basic concepts and experimental practices of a scientific discipline, as described by Thomas Kuhn, leading to a new way of understanding and investigating the world.

Parallel Computing: A computing paradigm where multiple calculations or processes are carried out simultaneously, enabling faster processing and the solution of more complex problems.

Pattern Recognition: The ability of a system to identify recurring patterns in data, used extensively in machine learning and AI for tasks like image and speech recognition.

Phenomenology: A philosophical approach that focuses on the study of conscious experience from a first-person perspective, emphasizing the importance of subjective awareness and lived experience.

Philosophy: The study of fundamental questions about existence, knowledge, values, reason, mind, and language, seeking to understand the nature of reality and our place within it.

Physics: The natural science that studies matter, energy, motion, and force, seeking to understand the fundamental laws governing the universe.

Pilot-Wave Theory: An interpretation of quantum mechanics, also known as Bohmian Mechanics, that posits the existence of both particles and guiding waves that govern their motion, providing a deterministic alternative to standard quantum mechanics.

Post-Quantum Cryptography: Cryptographic methods designed to be secure against attacks by both classical and quantum computers, crucial for maintaining secure communication in the quantum age.

Predictive Policing: The use of data analysis and AI to predict and prevent crime, raising ethical concerns about bias, privacy, and potential for abuse.

Problem Space: The set of all possible states or solutions that a problem can have, used in AI to analyze and solve problems.

Quantum Algorithm: An algorithm designed to run on a quantum computer, exploiting quantum phenomena like superposition and entanglement to solve certain problems more efficiently than classical algorithms.

Quantum Annealing: A quantum computing technique used to find the minimum of a function, particularly useful for optimization problems.

Quantum Bayesianism (QBism): An interpretation of quantum mechanics that emphasizes the role of an agent's beliefs and experiences in understanding quantum states.

Quantum Computing: A type of computing that utilizes quantum mechanical phenomena such as superposition and entanglement to perform computations, offering the potential to solve certain problems that are intractable for classical computers.

Quantum Cryptography: The use of quantum mechanics to encrypt and transmit information securely, offering the potential for unbreakable encryption.

Quantum Darwinism: A theory that explains how the classical world emerges from the quantum world by describing how certain quantum states are more likely to survive decoherence and be observed.

Quantum Entanglement: See Entanglement.

Quantum Field Theory (QFT): A theoretical framework that combines quantum mechanics with special relativity to describe the behavior of subatomic particles and fields.

Quantum Information Theory: The study of information processing in the context of quantum mechanics, exploring how quantum phenomena can be used to store, transmit, and manipulate information.

Quantum Logic: A system of logic that is different from classical logic and is used to reason about quantum phenomena, accommodating superposition and uncertainty.

Quantum Mechanics: The branch of physics that deals with the behavior of matter and energy at the atomic and subatomic levels, where classical physics breaks down.

Quantum Non-Locality: See Non-Locality.

Quantum Randomness: The inherent unpredictability in quantum events, as opposed to the deterministic nature of classical physics.

Quantum Supremacy: The point at which a quantum computer can solve a problem that no classical computer can solve in any feasible amount of time, demonstrating the computational advantage of quantum computers.

Qubit: The fundamental unit of quantum information, analogous to a bit in classical computing. Unlike classical bits that are limited to either 0 or 1, qubits can exist in multiple states simultaneously due to superposition and can be entangled with other qubits.

Rationalism: A philosophical view that knowledge comes primarily from reason and innate ideas rather than sensory experience, emphasizing the role of logic and deduction.

Reductionism: A philosophical approach that seeks to explain complex phenomena by breaking them down into simpler, more fundamental components, often used in science to understand systems.

Relational Quantum Mechanics (RQM): An interpretation of quantum mechanics, developed by

Carlo Rovelli, that proposes quantum states are not intrinsic properties of systems but describe relationships between them, emphasizing the role of the observer in defining quantum states.

Reverse Engineering: The process of analyzing a system or device to understand its design and function, often with the goal of reproducing it or creating a similar product.

Robotics: The branch of technology that deals with the design, construction, operation, and application of robots.

Sapience: The capacity for wisdom, reflective thought, and understanding.

Schrödinger's Equation: A fundamental equation in quantum mechanics that describes the evolution of a quantum system over time.

Science Fiction: A genre of fiction that explores speculative and imaginative concepts such as advanced technology, time travel, parallel universes, and extraterrestrial life.

Scientific Method: A systematic approach to acquiring knowledge that involves observation, hypothesis formulation, experimentation, and analysis.

Self-Awareness: The ability to perceive oneself as an individual, separate from the environment and other individuals, and to reflect on one's own existence and consciousness.

Self-Organization: The process by which complex patterns and structures emerge in a system without external control or guidance.

Semantics: The study of meaning in language, concerned with the relationships between words, symbols, and their interpretations.

Sentience: The capacity to experience feelings and sensations.

Singularity: A hypothetical point in the future where technological growth becomes uncontrollable and irreversible, resulting in unfathomable changes to human civilization.

Social Constructivism: A sociological theory that emphasizes the role of social interaction and cultural context in shaping knowledge, meaning, and reality.

Sociobiology: The study of the biological basis of social behavior.

Sociology: The study of human society, including social structures, institutions, and relationships.

Software Engineering: The application of engineering principles to the design, development, testing, and maintenance of software systems.

Solipsism: The philosophical view that only one's own mind is sure to exist.

Spacetime: The concept in physics that combines the three dimensions of space with the dimension of time into a single four-dimensional continuum.

Special Relativity: Einstein's theory that describes the relationship between space and time, and how they are perceived differently by observers in relative motion.

Strong AI: See Artificial General Intelligence (AGI).

Superposition: A quantum phenomenon where a particle can exist in multiple states simultaneously. For example, a qubit can be in a superposition of both 0 and 1 until measured.

Superdeterminism: A deterministic interpretation of quantum mechanics that rejects the assumption of independent measurements, suggesting that all events, including measurements, are predetermined.

Symbolic AI: An approach to AI that uses symbols and rules to represent knowledge and perform reasoning, in contrast to connectionist AI which uses neural networks.

Syntax: The study of the rules governing the structure of language, including the arrangement of words and phrases in sentences.

Systems Theory: An interdisciplinary field that studies systems as a whole, focusing on the interactions and relationships between their components.

Technological Determinism: The belief that technology is the primary driver of social and cultural change, shaping human behavior and values.

The Computational Paradigm: The idea that the universe fundamentally operates as a giant computer, processing information.

Theism: The belief in the existence of God or gods.

Theory of Everything: A hypothetical theory in physics that would unify all fundamental forces and particles of nature into a single framework.

Thermodynamics: The branch of physics that deals with heat, work, and temperature, and their relation to energy, entropy, and the physical properties of matter.

Thought Experiment: A hypothetical scenario used to explore the consequences of a theory or principle.

Transhumanism: A movement that advocates for the use of science and technology to overcome human limitations and enhance human capabilities, potentially leading to radical changes in the human condition.

Turing Test: A test, proposed by Alan Turing, of a machine's ability to exhibit intelligent behavior indistinguishable from that of a human. A machine passes the Turing test if a human evaluator cannot reliably distinguish between the machine's responses and those of a human.

Uncertainty Principle: See Heisenberg Uncertainty Principle.

Virtual Reality (VR): A technology that creates immersive, simulated environments, often used for entertainment, training, and therapy.

Von Neumann Architecture: A computer architecture that uses a single address space for both instructions and data.

Wave Function: In quantum mechanics, a mathematical description of the state of a quantum system, representing the probability of finding a particle in a particular state.

Weak AI: See Narrow AI.

References

Aaronson S., & Kuperberg G. (2023). *Quantum Computing Since Democritus*. Cambridge University Press.

Aspuru-Guzik, A. (2021). *Quantum computing for chemistry and materials science*. ACS Central Science, 7(2), 171-179.

Barad, K. (2007). *Meeting the Universe Halfway: Quantum Physics and the Entanglement of Matter and Meaning*. Duke University Press.

Bauman, Z. (2000). *Liquid Modernity*. Polity Press.

Benjamin, R. (2019). *Race After Technology: Abolitionist Tools for the New Jim Code*. Polity Press.

Bohr, N. (1934). *Atomic Theory and the Description of Nature*. Cambridge University Press.

Bostrom, N. (2005). *A history of transhumanist thought*. Journal of Evolution and Technology, 14(1), 1-30.

Bostrom, N. (2014). *Superintelligence: Paths, Dangers, Strategies*. Oxford University Press.

Bostrom, N., & Yudkowsky, E. (2022). *Ethics of Artificial Intelligence*. Cambridge University Press.

Brooks, R. A. (1991). *Intelligence without representation*. Artificial Intelligence, 47(1-3), 139-159.

Brown, B. (2012). *Daring Greatly: How the Courage to Be Vulnerable Transforms the Way We Live, Love, Parent, and Lead*. Gotham Books.

Campaign to Stop Killer Robots. (n.d.). *Home page*. Retrieved from https://www.stopkillerrobots.org/

Capra, F. (1975). *The Tao of Physics: An Exploration of the Parallels Between Modern Physics and Eastern Mysticism*. Shambhala Publications.

Carroll, S. (2019). *Something Deeply Hidden: Quantum Worlds and the Emergence of Spacetime*. Dutton.

Chalmers, D. J. (1995). *Facing up to the problem of consciousness. Journal of Consciousness Studies, 2*(3), 200-219.

Chung, S. (2018). *Drawing operations: Experiments in machine learning and co-creation. In Proceedings of the 2018 ACM SIGGRAPH Asia Symposium on Mobile Graphics and Interactive Applications* (pp. 1-2). ACM.

Cope, D. H. (1991). *Computers and Musical Style*. A-R Editions.

Dennett, D. C. (2003). *Freedom Evolves*. Viking.

Descartes, R. (2008). *Meditations on First Philosophy: With Selections from the Objections and Replies* (M. Moriarty, Trans.). Oxford University Press. (Original work published 1641)

Deutsch, D. (1985). *Quantum theory, the Church-Turing principle and the universal quantum computer.* Proceedings of the Royal Society of London. A. Mathematical and Physical Sciences, 400(1818), 97-117.

Deutsch, D., & Marletto, C. (2024). *The Science of Can and Can't: A Physicist's Journey Through the Land of Counterfactuals*. Penguin Books.

Dreyfus, H. L. (1992). *What Computers Still Can't Do: A Critique of Artificial Reason*. MIT Press.

Einstein, A., Podolsky, B., & Rosen, N. (1935*). Can quantum-mechanical description of physical reality be considered complete?* Physical Review, 47(10), 777-780.

Farahany, N. N. (2023). *The Battle for Your Brain: Defending the Right to Think Freely in the Age of Neurotechnology*. Doubleday.

Feynman, R. P., Leighton, R. B., & Sands, M. (1965). *The Feynman Lectures on Physics, Vol. 3: Quantum Mechanics*. Addison-Wesley.

Floridi, L. (2014). *The Fourth Revolution: How the Infosphere Is Reshaping Human Reality*. Oxford University Press.

Floridi, L. (2024). *The Ethics of Artificial Intelligence: Principles, Challenges, and Opportunities*. Oxford University Press.

Floridi, L., & Sanders, J. W. (2023). *Ethics of Artificial Intelligence and Emerging Technologies*. Oxford University Press.

Fukuyama, F. (2002). *Our Posthuman Future: Consequences of the Biotechnology Revolution*. Farrar, Straus and Giroux.

Gardner, H. (1983). *Frames of Mind: The Theory of Multiple Intelligences*. Basic Books.

Harari, Y. N. (2016). *Homo Deus: A Brief History of Tomorrow*. Harper.

Hick, J. (1966). *Evil and the God of Love*. Harper & Row.

Kant, I. (1996). *An answer to the question: What is enlightenment?* In M. J. Gregor (Ed.), *Immanuel Kant: Practical Philosophy* (pp. 11-22). Cambridge University Press. (Original work published 1784)

Kaye, D. (2019). *Report of the Special Rapporteur on the promotion and protection of the right to freedom of opinion and expression*. United Nations Human Rights Council. https://undocs.org/A/HRC/41/35

Koch, C. (2012). *Consciousness: Confessions of a Romantic Reductionist*. MIT Press.

Kuhn, T. S. (1962). *The Structure of Scientific Revolutions*. University of Chicago Press.

Kurzweil, R., & Diamandis P. H. (2024). *The Future is Faster Than You Think: How Converging Technologies Will Transform Business*. Simon & Schuster.

Lloyd, S. (2006). *Programming the Universe: A Quantum Computer Scientist Takes on Reality*. Alfred A. Knopf.

Maudlin, T. (2011). *Quantum Non-Locality and Relativity: Metaphysical Intimations of Modern Physics (3rd ed.)*. Blackwell Publishing.

Maudlin, T. (2019). *Philosophy of Physics: Quantum Theory*. Princeton University Press.

McKinsey & Company. (2023). *Quantum computing: What's real, what's hype, and what's next*. Retrieved from [www.mckinsey.com/insights/quantum-computing]

National Institute of Standards and Technology (NIST). (2022). *NIST Announces First Four Quantum-Resistant Cryptographic Algorithms*. Retrieved from [www.nist.gov/news-events/news/2022/07/nist-announces-first-four-quantum-resistant-cryptographic]

Nature. (2024). *Quantum machine learning: The next frontier in artificial intelligence.* Nature, 625(7993), S1-S4.

Nissenbaum, H. (2009). *Privacy in Context: Technology, Policy, and the Integrity of Social Life.* Stanford University Press.

Nussbaum, M. C. (2019). *The Monarchy of Fear: A Philosopher Looks at Our Political Crisis.* Simon & Schuster.

O'Neil, C. (2016). *Weapons of Math Destruction: How Big Data Increases Inequality and Threatens Democracy.* Crown.

Preskill, J. (2023). *Quantum Computing in Practice: From Theory to Application.* MIT Press.

Putnam, H. (1975). *The nature of mental states.* In *Mind, Language and Reality: Philosophical Papers, Vol. 2* (pp. 429-440). Cambridge University Press.

Rawls, J. (1971). *A Theory of Justice.* Harvard University Press.

Robinson, K. (2009). *The Element: How Finding Your Passion Changes Everything.* Viking.

Rovelli, C. (1996). *Relational quantum mechanics.* International Journal of Theoretical Physics, *35*(8), 1637-1678.

Rovelli, C. (2018*). Relational quantum mechanics.* In R. Batterman (Ed.), *The Oxford Handbook of Philosophy of Physics* (pp. 213-237). Oxford University Press.

Rovelli, C. (2023). *Helgoland: Making Sense of the Quantum Revolution.* Riverhead Books.

Russell, S., & Norvig, P. (2021). *Artificial Intelligence: A Modern Approach* (4th ed.). Pearson Education.

Russell, S., & Norvig, P. (2024). *Artificial Intelligence: A Modern Approach* (5th ed.). Pearson.

Sagan, C. (1980). *Cosmos.* Random House.

Schneier, B. (2018). *The Coming Crypto-Apocalypse.* IEEE Security & Privacy, 16(6), 70-73.

Searle, J. R. (1980). *Minds, brains, and programs.* Behavioral and Brain Sciences, *3*(3), 417-424.

Shearer, R. R. (2000). *Quantum mechanics and visual representation: Towards a new paradigm in art theory.* Leonardo, 33(1), 71-76.

Son, L. K., & Metcalfe, J. (2000). *Metacognitive and control strategies in study-time allocation.* Journal of Experimental Psychology: General, 129(2), 204-221.

Tegmark, M. (2014). *Our Mathematical Universe: My Quest for the Ultimate Nature of Reality*. Alfred A. Knopf.

Tegmark, M. (2021). *Life 3.0: Being Human in the Age of Artificial Intelligence*. Vintage Books.

Tononi, G. (2008). *Consciousness as integrated information: a provisional manifesto*. The Biological Bulletin, 215(3), 216-242

Turing, A. M. (1950). *Computing machinery and intelligence*. Mind, 59(236), 433-460.

Turkle, S. (2011). *Alone Together: Why We Expect More from Technology and Less from Each Other*. Basic Books.

Wheeler, J. A. (1990). *Information, physics, quantum: The search for links*. In W. H. Zurek (Ed.), *Complexity, entropy, and the physics of information* (pp. 3-28). Addison-Wesley Publishing Company.

World Economic Forum. (2023). *The Future of Jobs Report 2023*. https://www.weforum.org/reports/the-future-of-jobs-report-2023/

Zurek, W. H. (2024). *Decoherence and the Transition from Quantum to Classical*. Springer.

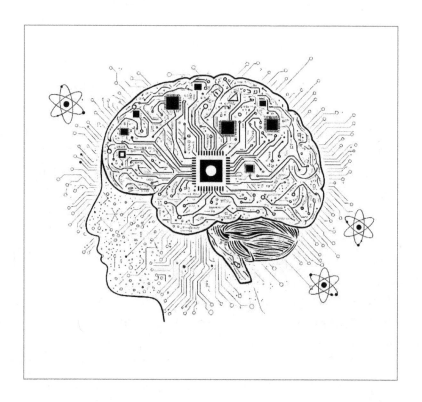

"In the dance of quantum entanglement,

we find an echo of our interconnectedness —

a reminder that humanity's fate

is woven into the fabric of existence."

- Ippolito, 2025